UNDER THE FIG TREE

CONVERSATIONS THAT AWAKEN THE POWER WITHIN AND TRANSFORM YOUR LIFE

Achieving Results That Matter

WILLIE C. HOOKS

Published by RICHER Press

An Imprint of Richer Life, LLC
5710 Ogeechee Road, Suite 200-175, Savannah, Georgia 31405
www.richerlifellc.com

Cover Design: RICHER Media

Volume book discounts are available for groups, companies and organizations. Contact the publisher for information and order instructions.

Library of Congress Control Number: 2025947491

UNDER THE FIG TREE
Conversations that Awaken the Power Within and Transform Your Life
Willie C. Hooks

1. Motivational Self-Help 2. Personal Transformation Self-Help 3. Happiness Self-Help

(pbk : alk. Paper)

ISBN: 979-89928996-4-1 Paperback

PRINTED IN THE UNITED STATES OF AMERICA

TABLE OF CONTENTS

4

Curious about the tree
on the front cover?

Buttress Roots and Monstrous Twisting Trunk of the Gigantic Moreton Bay Fig Tree

DEDICATION

I dedicate this book to the seekers—
To every soul who has wrestled with questions in the dark,
To those who have faced storms and still long for the light,
To the weary who carry burdens unseen,
And to the brave hearts who refuse to stop searching.

This book is also for the teachers and mentors—
Those who planted seeds of wisdom in silence,
Who listened more than they spoke,
Who pointed not to themselves but to the Source of all truth.

Finally, I dedicate this work to the One who meets us beneath the fig tree,
Who sees us fully, loves us wholly,
And whispers, *"Come, and I will give you rest."*

ACKNOWLEDGEMENTS

Thanks to all of my family, friends and associates for their contributions to multiple aspects of my life, and to my motivation to be in the position to leave this legacy of thought.

PROLOGUE

The Whisper Beneath the Leaves

Come closer, seeker.
Sit beneath the shade of this ancient tree.
Lay your burdens down upon the earth,
for it is strong enough to hold them.

Here, time slows.
The noise of the world fades into silence.
The shadows of your fears no longer chase you.
You are safe beneath these branches.

Do you feel the breeze? It carries truth.
Do you hear the rustling leaves? They echo wisdom.
Do you sense the stillness? It holds peace for your soul.

You have carried much—
the weight of work, of family, of love, of loss.
Your heart has known storms,
and yet here you are, still seeking.

This is holy ground.
Not because the tree is holy,
but because you are.

So, breathe deeply.
Release the voices that demand you prove yourself.
Release the fears that whisper you are not enough.
Release the past that clings too tightly.

Listen now—
for the voice you seek is not far.
It is here,
under the fig tree,
waiting for you.

A Winning Strategy For Accelerated Success

A POWERFUL STRATEGY FOR ACCELERATED SUCCESS is to begin every journey by reading, visualizing, and imprinting a Scripture Verse and a Reflective Prayer. These spiritual anchors set the tone, align your heart, and focus your mind.

Toward that end, take a moment now to read, visualize, and imprint the following:

Scripture Verse

"I saw you while you were still under the fig tree before Philip called you."
— John 1:48 (NIV)

Reflective Prayer

Lord, under this fig tree I bring You my restless heart.
Teach me to be still in Your presence.
Help me release the burdens I was never meant to carry,
and open my ears to hear Your whisper in the quiet.

Let these branches remind me that You see me,
even when I feel unseen.
Let this shade remind me that You protect me,
even when the world feels too harsh.
And let this moment remind me that I belong—
not because of what I do,
but because of who I am in You.

Here I rest.
Here I listen.
Here I am Yours.

Amen.

INTRODUCTION

EVENTUALLY, WE ALL COME TO A POINT where we look at the level of our results and the success we have achieved, and we begin to wonder: *How can I take my success to the next level?*
How can I achieve even greater results and success—without burning myself out?

These are the questions that mark a turning point: a desire not just for more, but for more with meaning, balance, and sustainability.

We wonder: *How do I master achievement—not as a one-time event, not as a fleeting accomplishment, but as a fruitful process fully integrated into the way I live and lead?*

Is there a sequence, a set of steps I can follow—a systematic way—that will elevate not just my results, but also my impact, my fulfillment, and my contribution?

And perhaps the most important question of all: *Is there more to life than this?*

The truth is, yes—there is more. More to achieve. More to give. More to become. But the next level of success is not found in working harder, chasing faster, or striving endlessly. It is found in mastering ourselves—our mindset, our discipline, our focus, and our ability to align who we are with what we do.

Our challenge is not simply to perform; it is to *transform*. To build achievement into the fabric of how we operate. To create success that is sustainable, meaningful, and deeply integrated with our values.

And that begins with a choice. A choice to stop chasing success as a distant prize—and instead, to embody success as a way of life.

This book was born from such questions. Beneath the branches of the Fig Tree—an ancient symbol of peace, rest, and divine encounter—seekers come to meet the Master. Through dialogue, reflection, prayer, and scripture, each chapter in this powerful life changing book unfolds as a sacred conversation between a struggling soul and a wise guide.

The seeker's challenges are not unfamiliar: low productivity, lack of achievement, poor time management, procrastination, and the frustration of not reaching the level of success they long for. These are the very struggles you may be carrying as you turn these pages. Yet here, in this space, you will discover that even the heaviest burdens can be transformed into stepping-stones of growth.

This is not just a book of teachings; it is an invitation. Each chapter offers dialogue rich with insight, a reflective question for you to wrestle with, practices to integrate into your daily life, affirmations to anchor truth, and a prayer with scripture to guide your spirit.

Come as you are. Bring your pain, your questions, and your longing. Sit under the fig tree. And as you listen to the voices within these pages, may you discover not only wisdom for life's challenges but also peace, renewal, and the courage to step into the life you were created to live.

How the Book Is Organized

A Proven Pathway to Lasting Success

This book is structured into three distinct parts, each representing a crucial phase in the journey toward greater results, achievement, success, contribution, and fulfillment. The sequence is intentional and designed to guide you step-by-step through the inner work required to master your life—starting with your personal habits and mindset, and culminating in your alignment with the greater universal flow.

Together, these three parts form a powerful blueprint for personal transformation and accelerated success.

Part I: Mastering Personal Effectiveness

Your journey begins with the mastery of *Personal Effectiveness*—the foundation of all achievement.
This section focuses on building essential skills and capabilities such as:

- Goal setting
- Time management
- Eliminating procrastination

When you address the mastery of these areas, you dramatically improve your ability to follow through with clarity and purpose. As a result, your capacity for achievement and lasting success begins to expand exponentially.

Part II: Rewiring the Mind Through Neuroplasticity

The second part of your journey focuses on the *Mind*—specifically, how to rewire and reprogram your thinking using the principles of neuroplasticity.

Here, you will learn how to:

- Identify and change limiting beliefs
- Develop new empowering habits
- Build emotional resilience

By intentionally reshaping your inner dialogue, you will unlock more of your potential and establish new pathways for sustainable growth, confidence, and fulfillment.

Part III: Aligning with the Universal Laws

The final section teaches you how to live in *alignment with Universal Laws*—timeless spiritual principles that govern abundance, manifestation, and fulfillment.

In this part, you will explore laws such as:

- The Law of Vibration
- The Law of Creation
- The Law of Attraction

By mastering these laws, life begins to flow with greater ease. You stop pushing and striving and instead tap into the natural rhythm of abundance, prosperity and wealth that is always available to those who align with it.

The Pathway Is Intentional

Each part of this book is built upon the previous one. It begins with personal mastery, expands into mental transformation, and culminates with spiritual alignment. Together, they form a complete system designed to elevate every dimension of your life.

This is not just a book of theory. It is a *guidebook for living*.
Let the conversations with the Master—and the insights they spark—lead you into a life of deeper meaning, greater impact, and lasting fulfillment.

THE FIRST AREA OF MASTERY
PART I
MASTERING PERSONAL EFFECTIVENESS
The Foundation of Lasting Success

THE FIRST AREA OF MASTERY begins with the self. *Personal effectiveness* is not just about productivity or time management—it is the very bedrock upon which all achievement, growth, and transformation are built. Without mastering this inner realm, even the grandest visions remain out of reach, lost to distraction, poor habits, or wavering commitment.

When you develop *personal effectiveness*, you do not just gain control over your schedule—you reclaim authorship over your life. It is here that discipline becomes devotion. Focus becomes fuel. And action, when aligned with clarity, begins to create compounding results that ripple through every dimension of your being.

Now, the Master gathers the seekers and speaks with quiet conviction. His message is simple, yet profound: Before you can build anything lasting, you must build yourself. The foundation of personal effectiveness—clarity, consistency, focus, and ownership—are not optional. They are essential. Without them, goals remain hollow. With them, success becomes inevitable.

In the unfolding dialogues to come, you will journey with the Master and his students into the practical and spiritual dimensions of this foundational discipline. Each conversation will illuminate a vital truth, offering tools to strengthen your habits, sharpen your focus, and elevate your capacity to create.

And so, the seekers sit beneath the early morning sun, notebooks open, hearts ready. For what begins now is not a lesson in doing more—but a path toward being more. Within the stillness of these teachings, the true essence of personal effectiveness is revealed—one principle at a time.

CHAPTER 1

The Power of Goal Setting and Goal Achievement

Introduction

Vision without action remains a dream. The path to personal effectiveness begins with clear intention—knowing what you want and committing to the steps that lead you there. In this focused conversation, the Master helps the seeker understand that goals are not just outcomes; they are sacred promises to oneself. With clarity, discipline, and faith, goals become the blueprint through which desire is transformed into destiny.

Quote

"A goal is a signal to the universe that you are ready to act, ready to grow, and ready to receive."
—The Master

Dialogue: The Seeker and the Master

Seeker (Elias): Master, I have noticed something troubling. I start many things in life, but I rarely finish them. My dreams are many, but my achievements are few.

Master: Then you have dreams, but not goals, Elias.

Elias: Is there truly such a difference?

Master: Yes. A dream is like the wind—beautiful but unfocused. A goal is like the sail that catches the wind and directs it forward. Without the sail, the wind scatters aimlessly.

Elias: So, my life lacks direction because I never set true goals?

Master: Exactly. A goal is a dream with clarity, a plan, and a date. If you say, "I want to be healthy," that is a wish. But if you say, "I will walk five miles a week and eat nourishing food," that is a goal.

Elias: But what about obstacles? They always come and break my progress.

Master: Obstacles are part of the journey. A clear goal keeps you steady when storms arise. If your eyes are on the destination, the waves will not frighten you.

Elias: And how do I know which goals are worthy?

Master: Ask: Does this goal align with your values? Does it serve your higher purpose? Goals built only on ego crumble. But goals built on service, growth, and God's will endure.

Elias: Then once I set a goal, how do I ensure I achieve it?

Master: You must master a process. Let me show you:

1. **Set a Desirable Goal** – Choose a goal worth pursuing, one that excites you and aligns with your values.
2. **Make it a SMART Goal** – Specific, Measurable, Attainable, Relevant, and Time-bound. For example, instead of saying, *"I want to save money,"* say, *"I will save $5,000 within 12 months by setting aside $100 each week."*
3. **Make a Plan** – Write down the steps you will take. Break the goal into milestones.
4. **Plan Your Work** – Use your calendar. Time-block specific hours to work on your goal. Protect these blocks as sacred appointments with your future.

5. **Work Your Plan** – When the time block arrives, act with discipline. Do not wait for motivation—faithful action creates momentum.
6. **Check Your Results** – At regular intervals, review your progress. Ask: What worked? What did not?
7. **Modify and Repeat** – Adjust the plan, refine your actions, and repeat the process until the goal is achieved.

Elias: That is clear and practical. But what if I fail again?

Master: Failure is feedback, not the end. Review, adjust, and press on. Each attempt strengthens your discipline and shapes your character. Remember, Elias, the goal shapes you more than you shape it. In pursuing it, you grow into the person God designed you to be.

Scripture Verse

"Write the vision; make it plain on tablets, so he may run who reads it."
– Habakkuk 2:2 (ESV)

"Commit to the Lord whatever you do, and he will establish your plans."
– Proverbs 16:3 (NIV)

Reflective Prayer

Heavenly Father,
Grant me the discipline to set goals that honor You,
The courage to pursue them despite obstacles,
And the wisdom to align my desires with Your will.
Help me to write the vision clearly,
To plan my work and work my plan,

To check my progress with humility,
And to press on until the purpose is fulfilled.
Amen.

Try This: *7-Day Goal Setting and Execution Challenge*

1. **Day 1 – Write One SMART Goal**: Choose a goal that is Specific, Measurable, Attainable, Relevant, and Time-bound. Write it down clearly.
2. **Day 2 – Break it Down**: Identify 3–5 milestones needed to achieve the goal.
3. **Day 3 – Make the Plan**: For each milestone, write the specific actions required.
4. **Day 4 – Time-Block**: Schedule these actions into your calendar. Protect those blocks as commitments.
5. **Day 5 – Act**: Begin working your plan during the scheduled time block. Focus on completion, not perfection.
6. **Day 6 – Review**: Ask yourself, *what worked? What did not?* Adjust your plan if necessary.
7. **Day 7 – Repeat**: Recommit to the process and take the next step forward

Goal: By the end of five days, you will have trained yourself to move from intention to action.

Affirmation to Anchor the Master's Teachings

"I set clear goals with purpose and take consistent steps toward them. I am focused, disciplined, and fully committed to achieving what I have been called to accomplish."

CHAPTER 2

Time Management and Demands

Introduction

Time is not something to be managed—it is something to be honored. In a world overflowing with noise and demands, the truly effective learn to protect what is sacred: their focus, their energy, and their priorities. In this timely teaching, the Master guides the seeker to see that time is not the enemy, but the canvas upon which a meaningful life is painted. How we spend it reveals what we truly value.

Quote

"You do not manage time—you master your attention, your choices, and your presence within it."
—The Master

Dialogue: The Seeker and the Master

Seeker (Caleb): Master, I feel like I am drowning. My days are packed with meetings, phone calls, errands, and endless to-do lists. No matter how much I do, there is always more. I feel constantly behind.

Master: Caleb, you are not drowning in time. You are drowning in choices. Every demand on your life is not a true priority. Tell me, do you own your time, or does your time own you?

Caleb: It feels like my time owns me. I wake up already behind, rush through the day, and collapse into bed wondering where the hours went.

Master: That is because you confuse activity with productivity. Running faster in the wrong direction does not get you closer to your destination. You must choose what matters most and release what does not.

Caleb: But Master, people depend on me. If I start saying no, won't I disappoint them?

Master: The greatest disappointment is not to others but to your own destiny. Every yes to what does not matter is a no to your calling. Time is life's most precious currency. Spend it only where it multiplies purpose, not where it drains you.

Caleb: So, I need to focus on my top priorities?

Master: Exactly. Begin by asking, "What three things, if accomplished today, would make the greatest difference?" Do those first. Then, guard your energy by creating rhythms of rest, focus, and renewal.

Caleb: That sounds good, but distractions pull me away.

Master: Then train your focus like a muscle. Set boundaries. Turn off the noise. Schedule your priorities instead of prioritizing your schedule. And always remember—your worth is not measured by how busy you are but by how intentional you are.

The Master's Process for Managing Time and Demands

1. **Set Clear Priorities** – At the start of each day, write down your top three tasks. Ask yourself, *"If I do only these three, will my day still matter?"* Let them guide you.

2. **Use Time-Blocking** – Assign specific blocks of time in your calendar for these tasks. Protect them as sacred appointments with your future.

3. **Eliminate the Trivial** – Learn to say no gracefully. Remember: every yes to something unimportant is a no to your true calling.

4. **Work the Plan** – When the time block arrives, focus deeply. Shut off distractions. Multitasking scatters the mind—focus multiplies results.

5. **Check and Adjust** – At the end of the day, review: What did I complete? What stole my time? What can I adjust tomorrow?

6. **Repeat Daily** – Consistency builds mastery. When practiced faithfully, these steps free you from pressure and give you power over your time.

Scripture Verse

"Teach us to number our days, that we may gain a heart of wisdom."
– Psalm 90:12 (NIV)

"Be very careful, then, how you live—not as unwise but as wise, making the most of every opportunity, because the days are evil."
– Ephesians 5:15–16 (NIV)

Reflective Prayer

Lord of time and eternity,
I confess I have been swept away by busyness,
trading focus for distraction, and peace for pressure.
Teach me to number my days with wisdom,
to choose what matters most,
and to release what does not serve Your purpose in me.
Give me strength to say no to the trivial,
and courage to say yes to the eternal.
In Your order and rhythm, let me find rest and power.
Amen.

Try This: *5-Day Time Mastery Practice*

1. **Choose Your Top 3** – Each morning, write down the three most important tasks for the day. Ask: *"If I only finish these three, will my day still matter?"*

2. **Time-Block** – Schedule specific blocks of time in your calendar to complete these tasks. Treat these blocks like sacred appointments you cannot cancel.

3. **Eliminate One Distraction** – For these five days, silence one common distraction during your focus blocks (social media, unnecessary email, or constant notifications).

4. **Review Nightly** – At the end of each day, review: *Did I complete my Top 3? What distracted me? What worked well?* Write this down.

5. **Refine and Repeat** – After five days, review your notes. Notice patterns. Keep what worked, adjust what did not, and recommit for the next week.

Goal: By the end of five days, you will have trained your focus, practiced discipline, and created a rhythm of intentional living.

Affirmation to Anchor the Master's Teachings

"I manage my time with wisdom and intention. I prioritize what matters most and create space for what brings peace, purpose, and productivity."

Quote

"Every time you postpone your purpose; you teach yourself that your dreams can wait. But they are waiting on you."

—The Master

CHAPTER 3

The Thief of Time: Procrastination

Introduction

Procrastination wears many disguises: fear, perfectionism, doubt, and distraction. But beneath them all lies the quiet resistance to becoming who we are meant to be. In this revealing dialogue, the Master helps the seeker confront the hidden cost of delay—not just in missed opportunities, but in lost self-trust. To overcome procrastination is to reclaim your power, your time, and your life.

Dialogue: The Seeker and the Master

Seeker (Caleb): Master, I find myself constantly delaying the things I know I need to do. I put off tasks at work, in my home, even in my personal growth. Instead of moving forward, I keep finding excuses or distractions. Why do I do this to myself?

Master: Caleb, procrastination is not simply about laziness. It is often fear dressed in delay. Fear of failure, fear of imperfection, fear of responsibility. Tell me, when you postpone these tasks, what is it you are truly avoiding?

Caleb: I suppose... I am afraid of starting and failing. If I do not begin, then I do not have to face that possibility.

Master: Yet by not beginning, you have already accepted failure. Procrastination is a silent thief—it steals time, confidence, and destiny. To conquer it, you must learn to act not when you feel ready, but when the call is before you.

Caleb: But I keep waiting for the right time, for better conditions.

Master: The right time is an illusion. Tomorrow is promised to no one. Small steps taken today are worth more than grand intentions left undone. Discipline is not about perfect timing; it is about faithful action.

Caleb: How do I strengthen myself to act when I feel resistance inside me?

Master: Break the mountain into stones. Do the smallest task first, for action builds momentum. And remember, procrastination weakens in the presence of purpose. When your "why" is clear, your "when" becomes now.

Seeker (Ethan): Master, I know what I should be doing, but I keep putting it off. I delay, I distract myself, I waste time. Then guilt comes, and I feel trapped in a cycle I cannot escape.

Master: Procrastination is not about laziness, Ethan—it is about fear. Fear of failure, fear of success, fear of discomfort. Your mind creates excuses to delay the very steps that would free you.

Ethan: That makes sense. I tell myself, "I'll do it later," but later rarely comes.

Master: Procrastination is the art of stealing from your future self. Each day you delay, you burden tomorrow with more weight. You must learn to honor the present moment, for it is the only place action exists.

Ethan: But how do I overcome this cycle?

Master: Begin with small, sacred steps. Do not wait for perfect conditions—they will never come. Do not wait for motivation—it comes after action, not before. Create a rhythm of discipline. Even ten minutes of focused effort plants seeds of momentum.

Ethan: So even if I cannot finish everything, I should start something?

Master: Exactly. Action breaks the spell of delay. When your ego whispers, *"Not now,"* you must respond, *"Now is the appointed time."*

Ethan: And what about the guilt I feel afterward?

Master: Replace guilt with grace. Yesterday is gone. Tomorrow is not promised. Today is your gift. Use it wisely, and procrastination will lose its power.

The Master's Process for Overcoming Procrastination

1. **Name the Fear** – Write down what you are avoiding and ask: *Am I afraid of failure, imperfection, or discomfort?* Naming the fear weakens its grip.
2. **Shrink the Task** – Break large goals into the smallest possible steps. Ask: *What is the smallest action I can take right now?*
3. **Time-Block Ten Minutes** – Commit to just ten minutes of action. Often, starting is all it takes to keep going.
4. **Eliminate Triggers** – Identify your top distractions and remove them during work time (silence notifications, clear your workspace, close extra tabs).
5. **Anchor to Purpose** – Remind yourself why this task matters and how it connects to your bigger goals or calling.
6. **Replace Guilt with Grace** – If you slip, do not condemn yourself. Reset and begin again.
7. **Repeat Daily** – Make this cycle a daily discipline until consistent action becomes your new habit.

Scripture Verse

"Do not boast about tomorrow, for you do not know what a day may bring."
– Proverbs 27:1 (NIV)

"Whatever your hand finds to do, do it with all you might."
– Ecclesiastes 9:10 (NIV)

Reflective Prayer

Lord of time and purpose,
I confess that I have delayed the work You have placed before me.
Forgive me for wasting the gift of today.
Give me courage to begin, strength to persist,
and wisdom to steward my time well.
Help me to honor You not with intentions,
but with faithful action.
Amen.

Try This: *5-Day Anti-Procrastination Challenge*

1. **Day 1 – Choose One Task**: Select a task you have been putting off. Commit to working on it for just 10 minutes.
2. **Day 2 – Break It Down**: Write the next three smallest steps for that task and do one.
3. **Day 3 – Eliminate One Distraction**: During your work block, silence a distraction you normally allow (like email or social media).
4. **Day 4 – Anchor Your Why**: Write down why this task matters and read it before starting.
5. **Day 5 – Reflect and Repeat**: At the end of the week, journal: *What progress did I make? What helped me act? What patterns do I need to change?*

Goal: By the end of five days, you will have disrupted the cycle of delay and built momentum toward consistent action.

Affirmation to Anchor the Master's Teachings

"I take action now. I release delay, doubt, and distraction. Every step I take moves me closer to my purpose with clarity and momentum."

Quote

"Excuses are the lies we sell to the self to avoid becoming who we were born to be."

—The Master

CHAPTER 4

Making Excuses:
The Chains of Self-Deception

Introduction

Excuses are the stories we tell ourselves to make comfort feel like courage. They soften the sting of inaction, but slowly tighten around our potential like invisible chains. In this honest conversation, the Master challenges the seeker to confront the subtle ways we deceive ourselves—disguising fear as logic, and limitation as reason. Freedom begins the moment we take full responsibility for the life we are creating.

Dialogue: The Seeker and the Master

Seeker (Adrian): Master, I want to improve my life, but it feels like circumstances always get in the way. I tell myself I will start tomorrow, but tomorrow never comes.

Master: Adrian, excuses are the lies we tell ourselves to stay comfortable. They are the cushions that protect us from effort, but they also keep us from growth.

Adrian: But sometimes my excuses feel true. I am tired, I am busy, I do not have the resources...

Master: Every excuse has a grain of truth, but truth twisted becomes bondage. The problem is not the obstacles—it is the story you wrap around them. You have made your limitations your shield instead of your stepping stones.

Adrian: Then what should I do when I feel weighed down by them?

Master: First, name them. Call the excuse what it is. Do not hide it in noble language. Say plainly, *"I did not act because I was afraid,"* or *"I delayed because I was lazy."* When excuses are exposed, they lose their power.

Adrian: That feels harsh.

Master: Honesty often does. But it is also liberating. Once you see excuses for what they are, you can replace them with responsibility. You must ask yourself: *"What can I do with what I have, right now?"*

Adrian: So, the cure for excuses is ownership?

Master: Exactly. Take ownership of your choices, your time, your gifts. Excuses will always present themselves, but you are not bound to them. The man who takes responsibility finds freedom—the man who makes excuses stays enslaved.

Seeker (Malik): Master, I have noticed that whenever I fall short, I am quick to explain why. *"I was too busy." "Others didn't help me." "The timing wasn't right."* I realize now I am full of excuses.

Master: Ah, Malik, excuses are the language of limitation. They comfort the ego but cripple the spirit. Every excuse is a small surrender of power.

Malik: But sometimes my reasons are true—life really is hard; people really do fail me.

Master: Yes, life can be hard. Others may fail you. But the question is—will you use those facts as stepping-stones or stumbling blocks? Excuses build walls; responsibility builds bridges.

Malik: So, Master, how do I stop making excuses?

Master: By embracing three practices:

1. **Take Radical Ownership** – Whatever the outcome, find your responsibility in it. Ownership breaks the excuse cycle.
2. **Turn Problems into Possibilities** – Every obstacle can be reshaped into an opportunity if you ask, *"What can I learn here?"*
3. **Speak Solutions, Not Excuses** – When tempted to excuse yourself, pause and instead declare what you will do differently.

Malik: That feels difficult.

Master: It is. But freedom lies on the other side. Excuses keep you bound to yesterday. Responsibility unlocks tomorrow.

The Master's Process for Breaking Excuses

1. **Identify the Excuse** – Write down the statement you tell yourself (e.g., *"I don't have time").*
2. **Expose the Truth Beneath It** – Ask, *"What am I really avoiding—fear, effort, or discomfort?"*
3. **Reframe the Story** – Replace the excuse with a statement of ownership (e.g., *"I didn't prioritize it today, but tomorrow I will block time for it.").*
4. **Choose Immediate Action** – Take one small step right away that proves the excuse wrong.
5. **Repeat with Discipline** – Each time an excuse arises, run it through this process until responsibility becomes your new habit.

Scripture Verse

"You, therefore, have no excuse, you who pass judgment on someone else, for at whatever point you judge another, you are condemning yourself, because you who pass judgment do the same things."
– Romans 2:1 (NIV)

Reflective Prayer

Lord,
Remove from me the habit of excuses.
Open my eyes to my own self-deception,
And give me courage to take ownership of my life.
Grant me strength to act in truth,
Discipline to rise above comfort,
And faith to step forward even when I feel unprepared.
Let my words be few, and my actions speak of my trust in You.
Amen.

Try This: *The No Excuse Journal*

1. For one week, carry a small notebook or use your phone.
2. Each time you hear yourself making an excuse (to yourself or others), write it down exactly as you said it.
3. At the end of the day, review your list. For each excuse, write a replacement statement of ownership (e.g., *"Excuse: I didn't have time. Truth: I chose not to use my time wisely."*).
4. Choose one action you can take the next day to prove the excuse false.
5. At the end of the week, reflect: How many excuses did I confront? What shifted in my mindset?

Goal: By tracking and replacing your excuses, you will begin to break free from self-deception and step into responsibility.

Affirmation to Anchor the Master's Teachings:

"I take full responsibility for my life. I release every excuse and choose action, truth, and growth over limitation and fear."

Quote

"To master your life, you must first master your insight. What you see within will shape everything around you."

—The Master

CHAPTER 5

Self-Awareness: Seeing Yourself with Clarity and Compassion

Introduction

Self-awareness is the foundation of growth. To lead yourself well, you must first know yourself well. Recognizing your strengths gives you confidence. Understanding your weaknesses gives you humility. Acknowledging your emotions gives you wisdom. In this revealing conversation, the Master helps the seeker develop the courage to look inward with honesty—not for judgment, but for alignment. With self-awareness comes power: the power to choose wisely, live intentionally, and set goals that reflect the truth of who you are.

Dialogue: The Seeker and the Master

Seeker (Samuel): Master, I am working hard to grow, but sometimes I feel lost. I do not know if I am making progress—or just pretending. How do I truly know myself?

Master: Samuel, the journey within is the most important journey you will ever take. Without self-awareness, even the best intentions drift off course.

Samuel: I think I know myself... but I do not always understand why I do what I do.

Master: That is the beginning of wisdom. To become effective, you must be reflective. Self-awareness is not just knowing your strengths—it is being honest about your habits, triggers, and thoughts. It is noticing your reactions and tracing them back to the beliefs that created them.

Samuel: So, it is not just about self-confidence?

Master: No. Self-awareness is deeper than confidence—it is clarity. Confidence without awareness becomes arrogance. But awareness breeds true authority, because it is rooted in truth.

Samuel: What should I be aware of?

Master: Three areas:

1. **Your Strengths** – What energizes you? What do others consistently seek from you?
2. **Your Weaknesses** – Where do you tend to avoid responsibility, break focus, or repeat mistakes?
3. **Your Emotions** – What patterns show up under pressure? What emotions visit you most often—and what are they trying to teach you?

Samuel: And once I am aware... what then?

Master: Then you set goals not based on fantasy, but on truth. You make decisions that honor your values. You communicate from a place of understanding, not assumption. You live as the observer, not the reactor.

The Master's Process for Developing Self-Awareness

1. **Daily Check-In** – Ask yourself each morning and evening: "What am I feeling? Why?" Name the emotions without judgment.
2. **Strengths Inventory** – List 5 activities that make you feel strong, energized, or fulfilled. Reflect on how you can do more of them.
3. **Weakness Reflection** – Identify 3 habits or behaviors that hold you back. Do not criticize—just notice. Awareness is the first step to change.
4. **Emotional Triggers Journal** – Keep track of moments you overreact or withdraw. What situations triggered you? What belief lies underneath?
5. **Seek Honest Feedback** – Ask a mentor or trusted friend: "What's one thing I do well?" and "What's one area I could grow in?"
6. **Align Goals to Identity** – Set personal goals that reflect your true self—not just who you think you should be, but who you are becoming.

Scripture Verse

"Search me, O God, and know my heart; test me and know my anxious thoughts."
—Psalm 139:23 (NIV)

"The purposes of a person's heart are deep waters, but one who has insight draws them out."
—Proverbs 20:5 (NIV)

Reflective Prayer

Father of Wisdom,
Teach me to see myself as You see me—

Not with shame, but with grace.
Help me notice my gifts,
Acknowledge my flaws,
And understand my emotions without fear.
Shine light on the blind spots of my soul.
May my self-awareness lead to humility,
My humility to growth,
And my growth to Your glory.
Amen.

Try This: *5-Day Self-Awareness Journal*

1. **Day 1 – Strengths Scan**
   Write down what you did well today. What felt natural? Where did you feel proud?

2. **Day 2 – Emotion Awareness**
   Name three emotions you felt today. What triggered them? How did you respond?

3. **Day 3 – Weakness Reflection**
   Where did you procrastinate, get distracted, or self-sabotage? Be honest, not harsh.

4. **Day 4 – Feedback Day**
   Ask someone close to you for one piece of feedback—what they admire in you and what they think you could improve.

5. **Day 5 – Identity-Aligned Goal**
   Set one new goal that aligns with your strengths and values—not someone else's expectations.

Goal: To develop the clarity and emotional intelligence that comes from knowing yourself deeply, so that your goals, decisions, and relationships reflect your truest self.

Affirmation to Anchor the Master's Teachings:

"I see myself clearly and compassionately. I honor my strengths, acknowledge my growth areas, and choose to live with honest alignment."

Quote

"Emotional intelligence is not the absence of emotion—it is the presence of wisdom in how you carry it."

—The Master

CHAPTER 6

Emotional Intelligence: Leading with Heart and Wisdom

Introduction

Emotional intelligence is the quiet strength that turns reaction into reflection and conflict into connection. It is more than just *"being nice"*—it is the ability to understand your own emotional landscape, manage your responses, and tune into the feelings of others. In this profound conversation, the Master guides the seeker through the art of self-regulation, empathy, and calm leadership. When you master your emotions, you create space for compassion, clarity, and deeper human connection.

Dialogue: The Seeker and the Master

Seeker (Samuel): Master, I often get overwhelmed by my emotions. One small thing can trigger me, and before I know it, I have said something I regret.

Master: Emotions are not your enemy, Samuel. They are messengers. But without understanding, they become masters instead of messengers. Emotional intelligence is the ability to receive the message without letting it dictate your behavior.

Samuel: So, it is not about suppressing how I feel?

Master: Never. Suppression is avoidance. Intelligence is awareness. You must learn to feel without being ruled by the feeling.

Samuel: That sounds difficult when I am under pressure—especially around other people.

Master: That is the test of mastery. Emotional intelligence has three dimensions:

1. **Self-awareness** – Knowing what you feel and why.
2. **Self-regulation** – Choosing your response instead of reacting impulsively.
3. **Empathy** – Understanding the emotional state of others, even when they cannot express it clearly.

Samuel: How do I develop these skills?

Master: By practicing pause. By becoming curious instead of defensive. And by seeing emotions not as flaws—but as indicators of what matters most. Your emotional patterns are not here to harm you—they are here to guide you.

Samuel: And how do I handle conflict?

Master: With calm. With listening. With the discipline to stay grounded even when others are not. The emotionally intelligent do not aim to win arguments—they aim to win understanding.

The Master's Process for Building Emotional Intelligence

1. **Practice the Pause** – When emotions rise, pause for 5 seconds. Take a deep breath. Let clarity catch up to emotion.
2. **Name the Feeling** – Say silently: "I feel angry." "I feel anxious." Naming emotion reduces its control.
3. **Ask the Root Question** – "Why am I feeling this way?" Trace it back to a thought, belief, or unmet need.
4. **Choose a Response** – Do not just react. Ask: "What would wisdom do here?" or "What outcome do I want to create?"

5. **Mirror Empathy** – In conflict, reflect the other person's emotion without judgment: "It sounds like you're frustrated." This builds trust.

6. **Repair Quickly** – When you make an emotional mistake, take responsibility and apologize with sincerity. Growth lies in the repair.

Scripture Verse

"A gentle answer turns away wrath, but a harsh word stirs up anger."
—Proverbs 15:1 (NIV)

"Whoever is slow to anger has great understanding, but he who has a hasty temper exalts folly."
—Proverbs 14:29 (ESV)

Reflective Prayer

God of Peace and Wisdom,
Teach me to understand the language of my emotions.
Give me the strength to pause,
The courage to reflect,
And the grace to respond with love.
When others are angry, help me be calm.
When I am hurt, help me seek healing—not harm.
Let my heart be tender, my mind be clear,
And my words be filled with truth and peace.
Amen.

Try This: *5-Day Emotional Intelligence Builder*

1. **Day 1 – Emotional Check-In**
   Pause three times during the day and ask, "What am I feeling right now?" Write it down.

2. **Day 2 – Response Review**
   At the end of the day, reflect: "Where did I react today? What could I have done differently?"

3. **Day 3 – Listen Without Defending**
   During one conversation, practice active listening. Do not interrupt. Do not defend. Just receive.

4. **Day 4 – Name & Reframe**
   When a negative emotion arises, name it and ask: "What positive action can I take from this feeling?"

5. **Day 5 – Empathy Practice**
   Choose one person to encourage or comfort today. Offer kindness, even if they seem distant or difficult.

Goal: To develop the awareness, regulation, and empathy necessary to navigate emotions with wisdom—leading to stronger relationships, better decisions, and a more peaceful inner life.

Affirmation to Anchor the Master's Teachings:

"I understand and manage my emotions with grace. I lead with empathy, respond with wisdom, and build deeper connections through compassion."

CHAPTER 7

Communication: Speaking with Clarity, Listening with Presence

Introduction

Communication is more than words—it is connection. The ability to speak with clarity and listen with intention is the foundation for trust, collaboration, and meaningful relationships. Whether in leadership, partnership, or friendship, those who communicate well build bridges where others build barriers. In this essential conversation, the Master teaches the seeker that effective communication starts not with the mouth, but with the heart—through presence, humility, and the willingness to truly understand.

Quote

"You cannot change what you do not understand—and you cannot understand what you do not hear."
—The Master

Dialogue: The Seeker and the Master

Seeker (Samuel): Master, I want to improve my communication. I sometimes feel misunderstood, or I say things that come out wrong. And honestly... I struggle to really listen when emotions are high.

Master: You are not alone, Samuel. Most people listen to reply, not to understand. And most speak to be heard, not to connect. True communication requires both clarity and compassion.

Samuel: So where do I start?

Master: Begin with two commitments:

1. **To express yourself with honesty and clarity.**
2. **To listen without defending or interrupting.**

Samuel: Listening is hard when I feel attacked or pressured.

Master: That is where growth begins. Listening is not agreement—it is acknowledgment. When you truly hear someone, you create space for resolution. And when you speak clearly and calmly, you create space for respect.

Samuel: What makes someone a great communicator?

Master: They do three things well:

- They **listen actively**—with their eyes, their ears, and their heart.
- They **speak clearly**—not to impress, but to express truth.
- They **check for understanding**—because they care more about clarity than being right.

Samuel: And what happens when I mess up—say the wrong thing?

Master: Then you return with humility. Communication is not about perfection. It is about intention. If your goal is connection — people will feel it—even when your words are not perfect.

The Master's Process for Effective Communication

1. **Be Fully Present** – Put down distractions. Make eye contact. Let your posture say, *"I'm here with you."*
2. **Listen to Understand** – Focus on the speaker's words, tone, and body language. Ask, *"What are they really trying to say?"*

3. **Pause Before You Speak** – Gather your thoughts. Breathe. Choose clarity over cleverness.
4. **Speak with Intention** – Use simple, honest language. Avoid blame. Speak from your own experience using "I" statements.
5. **Clarify, do not Assume** – Say: *"What I hear you saying is..."* or *"Can I make sure I understand you correctly?"*
6. **Respond, do not React** – Especially in conflict, respond from a calm place. Reacting is automatic. Responding is intentional.
7. **Close with Respect** – Whether you agree or disagree, end with appreciation: *"Thank you for sharing."*

Scripture Verse

"Let your conversation be always full of grace, seasoned with salt, so that you may know how to answer everyone."
—Colossians 4:6 (NIV)

"Everyone should be quick to listen, slow to speak and slow to become angry."
—James 1:19 (NIV)

Reflective Prayer

God of Wisdom and Words,
Help me to speak with truth and tenderness,
To listen with patience and presence.
Guard my tongue from harm,
And open my ears to what others cannot say aloud.
Let my words build bridges, not walls—
Let my silence hold space, not distance.
Make me a vessel of clarity,

And an agent of peace in every conversation.
Amen.

Try This: *5-Day Communication Challenge*

1. **Day 1 – Silent Listening**
   In one conversation, say less. Just listen. Notice what you hear when you are not thinking about your reply.

2. **Day 2 – "I" Statements Only**
   Speak using only "I" statements when discussing your feelings.
   Example: "I feel overlooked when..." instead of "You always ignore me."

3. **Day 3 – Mirror Back**
   In one conversation, reflect what you heard.
   "What I'm hearing is..." or "It sounds like you feel..."

4. **Day 4 – Clarify a Misunderstanding**
   Reach out to someone where there has been confusion or tension. Seek clarity and connection—not blame.

5. **Day 5 – Speak Your Appreciation**
   Tell one person something you have been meaning to say. Express gratitude or affirmation clearly and sincerely.

Goal: To strengthen your ability to communicate with clarity, empathy, and integrity—building deeper relationships and fostering greater collaboration in every area of your life.

Affirmation to Anchor the Master's Teachings:

"I speak with clarity and intention. I listen with presence and empathy. My words build trust, and my silence holds space for understanding."

CHAPTER 8

Adaptability: Growing Through Change with Grace

Introduction

Change is not the enemy of growth—it is its birthplace. The ability to adapt, to pivot when needed, and to learn from every new challenge is a hallmark of personal effectiveness and inner strength. In this timely dialogue, the Master helps the seeker embrace life's uncertainties, not with fear, but with faith. Those who adapt do not just survive change—they evolve through it. Flexibility, reflection, and resilience become their tools for transformation.

Quote

"It is not the strongest who thrive, but those most willing to grow when life changes course."
—The Master

Dialogue: The Seeker and the Master

Seeker (Samuel): Master, I have been feeling overwhelmed. Everything around me is shifting—my work, my relationships, even my routines. I feel like I am losing control.

Master: Samuel, change is not designed to weaken you. It is designed to awaken you. What feels like chaos is often the beginning of creation.

Samuel: But I like stability. I like knowing what to expect.

Master: Stability is comfortable—but it is not always where growth lives. Adaptability is the ability to move forward even when the ground beneath your moves. It is not weakness to bend—it is wisdom.

Samuel: So how do I become more adaptable? I cannot stop life from changing.

Master: You do not need to stop it. You need to meet it. Let experience become your teacher, not your tormentor. Ask:

- *What is this change asking of me?*
- *What new version of me is being called forth?*

Samuel: That sounds hard.

Master: It is—but it is holy work. The adaptable see every challenge as a classroom, every ending as an invitation, and every season as a lesson. They become students of transition—and masters of evolution.

The Master's Process for Strengthening Adaptability

1. **Accept the Shift** – Begin by saying: *"This is happening."* Resisting change drains energy. Acceptance frees it.
2. **Adjust Your Mindset** – Shift from *"Why is this happening to me?"* to *"What can I learn from this?"*
3. **Identify What You Can Control** – Even in chaos, you can choose your attitude, your words, your actions, and your next step.
4. **Learn in Real Time** – Journal your experiences. Ask: "What is this season teaching me about myself?"
5. **Stay Open to New Paths** – Do not cling to old ways out of fear. New routes often lead to better destinations.

6. **Practice Micro-Adapting** – Intentionally change small routines: take a different route to work, learn a new skill, or engage with different people to train your brain for flexibility.

Scripture Verse

"Forget the former things; do not dwell on the past. See, I am doing a new thing! Now it springs up—do you not perceive it?"
—Isaiah 43:18–19 (NIV)

"And we know that in all things God works for the good of those who love him, who have been called according to his purpose."
—Romans 8:28 (NIV)

Reflective Prayer

God of Seasons and Shifts,
Thank You for being unchanging when all around me changes.
Help me to meet change with grace,
To bend without breaking,
To trust when I cannot see,
And to grow through what I do not understand.
Teach me to release fear,
To welcome the unknown,
And to walk with faith into the new paths You are preparing.
Amen.

Try This: *5-Day Adaptability Growth Plan*

1. **Day 1 – Journal a Past Change**
   Reflect on a previous life change. What was difficult? What did you learn? How are you stronger now?

2. **Day 2 – Reframe a Current Challenge**
   Choose one situation that feels uncertain. Write 3 possible gifts or lessons hidden in it.

3. **Day 3 – Do Something New**
   Change one routine today. Take a new route, try a new food, or change your schedule slightly. Notice how you respond.

4. **Day 4 – Talk About Transition**
   Call someone and share how you are navigating change. Listening to another perspective builds insight and empathy.

5. **Day 5 – Set an Adaptability Intention**
   Write an "I will" statement that empowers flexibility.
   Example: "I will remain open, curious, and calm no matter what today brings."

Goal: To develop the mindset and habits of adaptability—allowing you to embrace change with courage, learn from every experience, and grow into the next version of yourself with resilience and grace.

Affirmation to Anchor the Master's Teachings:

"I embrace change with courage and flexibility. Every challenge is an opportunity to grow, evolve, and become more aligned with who I am called to be."

CHAPTER 9

Problem-Solving: Turning Obstacles into Opportunities

Introduction

Life will always present problems—but growth comes when we choose to face them with clarity, courage, and creativity. Problem-solving is not just a skill—it is a mindset. When we develop the ability to think critically, evaluate situations logically, and respond with resourceful action, we transform challenges into stepping-stones. In this empowering conversation, the Master shows the seeker how to see problems not as dead ends, but as divine

invitations to rise.

Quote

"Every problem carries a gift within it. The wise do not panic—they pause, ask, and proceed with purpose."
—The Master

Dialogue: The Seeker and the Master

Seeker (Samuel): Master, I feel stuck. Every time I try to move forward, something goes wrong—unexpected problems, setbacks, delays. It is like the path is blocked.

Master: Samuel, problems are not blocks. They are bridges in disguise. You are being invited to rise—to think, to stretch, and to trust.

Samuel: But I do not always know what to do. I get overwhelmed. My mind goes in circles.

Master: That is because you are trying to solve the problem with panic instead of process. True problem-solvers are calm explorers. They do not rush for answers—they ask the right questions.

Samuel: So, what is the process?

Master: There are three gates every problem must pass through:

1. **Observation** – What exactly is the problem?
2. **Evaluation** – What are the facts, and what are the assumptions?
3. **Innovation** – What are three creative ways to respond?

Samuel: And if none of that work?

Master: Then you learn, adjust, and try again. A problem is only a failure if you refuse to face it. But if you meet it with humility and persistence, it becomes a teacher.

The Master's Process for Effective Problem-Solving

1. **Define the Problem Clearly** – Ask: *What is happening? What outcome do I desire?* Be specific.
2. **Separate Facts from Feelings** – List what you know (facts) and what you believe or fear (feelings). This brings clarity.
3. **Brainstorm Without Limits** – Write down 3–5 possible solutions, even if some seem unconventional or risky. Creativity thrives in freedom.
4. **Evaluate the Options** – What are the potential consequences, benefits, and risks of each solution?
5. **Take Focused Action** – Choose one option and take the first step. Action dissolves anxiety.

6. **Reflect and Adjust** – If it works, build on it. If not, reflect on what you learned and try a new approach.

Scripture Verse

"If any of you lacks wisdom, you should ask God, who gives generously to all without finding fault, and it will be given to you."
—James 1:5 (NIV)

"Trust in the Lord with all your heart and lean not on your own understanding; in all your ways submit to him, and he will make your paths straight."
—Proverbs 3:5–6 (NIV)

Reflective Prayer

God of Wisdom and Light,
When I face problems,
Calm my heart and clear my mind.
Teach me to see with truth,
To think with creativity,
And to act with courage.
Help me welcome each challenge
As an invitation to grow.
Let my solutions reflect Your wisdom,
And my actions bring peace and progress.
Amen.

Try This: *5-Step Problem-Solving Reflection*

1. **Identify a Current Challenge** – Write down one unresolved problem you are facing.
2. **List the Facts** – What do you *know* to be true? What is fear or assumption?

3. **Brainstorm 3 Solutions** – Push yourself to go beyond the obvious. Do not judge—just create.
4. **Choose One and Act** – Take one small action toward the solution today. Just one.
5. **Journal What You Learned** – What surprised you? What would you do differently next time?

Goal: To strengthen your critical thinking and creative problem-solving skills — empowering you to approach every challenge with clarity, courage, and the confidence that no obstacle is bigger than your willingness to grow.

Affirmation to Anchor the Master's Teachings:

"I face every challenge with clarity, creativity, and calm. I am a solution-bringer, turning obstacles into stepping-stones for growth and progress."

CHAPTER 10

Self-Discipline and Consistency: Building the Bridge Between Desire and Destiny

Introduction

Desire starts the journey, but discipline carries it forward. Without consistent action, even the clearest goals fade into distant wishes. Self-discipline is the quiet power behind success—the ability to do what must be done, even when you do not feel like it. In this transformational dialogue, the Master teaches the seeker how to build habits, maintain focus, and overcome the gravitational pull of procrastination. When discipline becomes a way of life, progress becomes inevitable.

Quote

"Consistency is more powerful than intensity. A small act repeated with discipline becomes the force that shapes your future."
—The Master

Dialogue: The Seeker and the Master

Seeker (Samuel): Master, I have so many dreams—but I keep getting in my own way. I start strong, but I do not follow through. I get distracted, I lose focus... and then I feel guilty for quitting.

Master: You are not failing because your dream is too big, Samuel. You are struggling because your discipline is too small. Motivation is loud—but discipline is loyal.

Samuel: But I do not always feel inspired. Some days I just do not have the energy.

Master: That is when it matters most. True discipline is not about feelings—it is about decision. And decision, practiced daily, becomes habit.

Samuel: So, what is the secret to consistency?

Master: The secret is to stop waiting for the perfect moment—and to start honoring small, daily progress. Discipline is not about perfection. It is about showing up, again, until showing up becomes who you are.

Samuel: And how do I defeat procrastination?

Master: You make it harder to delay and easier to start. You simplify your tasks, create rituals, remove distractions, and remind yourself: *I keep promises to myself.* Every time you follow through, you rebuild trust with your future.

The Master's Process for Self-Discipline and Consistency

1. **Start with One Clear Goal** – Choose a single focus. Write it down. Be specific. Discipline thrives in simplicity.
2. **Build Micro-Habits** – Break the goal into small, daily actions. *Example: Instead of "write a book," start with "write 100 words a day."*
3. **Create a Trigger Routine** – Anchor your habit to something you already do. *Example: "After I brush my teeth, I journal for 5 minutes."*
4. **Remove Friction** – Eliminate distractions. Set up your environment to make the desired action easy to begin.

5. **Track Your Wins** – Use a visual tracker (calendar, journal, app) to see your consistency. Progress breeds motivation.
6. **Forgive, Then Restart** – Missed a day? Do not quit—reset. The disciplined are not perfect, but they are persistent.

Scripture Verse

"No discipline seems pleasant at the time, but painful. Later, however, it produces a harvest of righteousness and peace for those who have been trained by it."
—Hebrews 12:11 (NIV)

"Whoever can be trusted with very little can also be trusted with much..."
—Luke 16:10 (NIV)

Reflective Prayer

God of Order and Strength,
Teach me to be faithful in the small things,
To show up when it is hard,
To follow through when I feel weak,
And to trust that You bless every honest effort.
Shape my habits with heaven's discipline,
And let my consistency become a testimony
Of Your power working through me.
Amen.

Try This: *5-Day Self-Discipline Builder*

1. **Day 1 – Identify the Keystone Habit**
   Choose one habit that, if done daily, would create momentum. Write it down.

2. **Day 2 – Start with 5 Minutes**
   Do that habit today—for just 5 minutes. The goal is consistency, not perfection.

3. **Day 3 – Set a Trigger**
   Pick a daily action to link the habit to. Example: "Right after lunch, I stretch for 5 minutes."

4. **Day 4 – Eliminate One Distraction**
   Turn off one notification, close one tab, or remove one habit that steals your focus.

5. **Day 5 – Reflect and Reset**
   How did it feel to follow through? Where did you struggle? How can you simplify the process moving forward?

Goal: To strengthen your capacity for follow-through by developing small, repeatable habits rooted in discipline—so that consistency becomes your superpower and your dreams become your daily reality.

Affirmation to Anchor the Master's Teachings:

"I am disciplined, focused, and consistent. I honor my goals with daily action, and my steady steps are building the life I envision."

CHAPTER 11

Leadership and Influence: Inspiring Trust, Elevating Others

Introduction

Leadership is not about titles—it is about trust. Influence is not about control—it is about contribution. True leaders inspire by who they are, not just by what they do. They take initiative, serve others, and lift those around them. In this transformative dialogue, the Master shows the seeker that leadership begins with character, deepens through consistency, and multiplies through service. When you lead with integrity, your influence becomes a legacy.

Quote

"Leadership is not the power to command—it is the courage to serve, the clarity to guide, and the humility to lift others higher than yourself."
—The Master

Dialogue: The Seeker and the Master

Seeker (Samuel): Master, I have always thought leadership was for people in charge—CEOs, managers, pastors. But lately I feel like I am being called to lead... and I am not sure I am ready.

Master: Samuel, leadership is not a position. It is a posture of the heart. You lead the moment someone looks to you for direction, support, or example.

Samuel: So, anyone can lead?

Master: Everyone does lead—either by intention or by neglect. Your influence is always at work. The question is: What are you influencing, and how?

Samuel: That is a big responsibility.

Master: Yes. But it begins with small actions. The most powerful leaders lead themselves well. They take responsibility, speak with integrity, follow through on their word, and inspire trust through consistency.

Samuel: And how do I grow in influence?

Master: Three ways:

1. **Earn trust by being trustworthy.**
2. **Help others grow.**
3. **Lead from within before leading outward.**

When people feel seen, supported, and strengthened by you—they follow not because they must, but because they want to.

Samuel: What if I do not feel qualified?

Master: You do not need to be perfect. You need to be present, purposeful, and committed to becoming. Leadership is not about being the best—it is about helping others become their best.

The Master's Process for Growing Leadership and Influence

1. **Lead Yourself First** – Start with discipline, accountability, and vision in your own life. Others will mirror what you model.
2. **Inspire Trust** – Be reliable, honest, and humble. Influence flows from character more than charisma.

3. **Take Initiative** – Do not wait for permission to add value. Leaders rise by solving problems, not avoiding them.
4. **Empower Others** – Listen. Encourage. Develop the gifts in others. Make space for their growth.
5. **Speak with Vision** – Great leaders point to what is possible. Use words that uplift, unite, and ignite belief.
6. **Serve from the Heart** – Leadership is service in action. The more you serve, the more people want to follow.

Scripture Verse

"Whoever wants to become great among you must be your servant."
—Matthew 20:26 (NIV)

"The integrity of the upright guides them, but the unfaithful are destroyed by their duplicity."
—Proverbs 11:3 (NIV)

Reflective Prayer

Lord of Light and Leadership,
Teach me to lead not for power, but for purpose.
May I inspire trust by walking in truth,
Take initiative when others hesitate,
And lift others even as I grow.
Let my influence be rooted in service,
My words speak life,
And my actions build something eternal.
Make me a leader who reflects You.
Amen.

Try This: ***5-Day Leadership Builder***

1. **Day 1 – Lead Yourself**
   Identify one area of your life that needs more discipline or clarity. Take one step toward alignment.

2. **Day 2 – Speak Life into Someone**
   Encourage or affirm someone today. Let them know how they inspire you.

3. **Day 3 – Ask and Listen**
   Ask someone how they are doing or what they need—and really listen. Leadership begins with empathy.

4. **Day 4 – Solve a Problem**
   Look for a small problem at work, home, or in your community. Take initiative to offer a solution or lend support.

5. **Day 5 – Reflect on Legacy**
   Write down what kind of leader you want to be remembered as. What values will guide your influence?

Goal: To grow as a trusted, service-oriented leader who inspires, uplifts, and multiplies their influence through integrity, action, and heart-centered contribution.

Affirmation to Anchor the Master's Teachings:

"I lead with integrity, serve with humility, and inspire trust through my actions. My influence lifts others and leaves a legacy of purpose."

THE SECOND AREA OF MASTERY
THE FIRST AREA OF MASTERY
PART II
REWIRING THE MIND
Awakening the Power of Neuroplasticity

THE SECOND AREA OF MASTERY invites us inward—to the unseen architecture of thought. Here, in the vast and malleable landscape of the mind, lies the power to reshape your reality. Through the science of neuroplasticity, you can break free from outdated

patterns, release limiting beliefs, and create new mental pathways that support clarity, confidence, and growth.

Rewiring the mind is not a one-time shift, but a conscious practice—a daily return to possibility. By intentionally choosing new thoughts, you recondition the nervous system to expect abundance, pursue goals with certainty, and recover from setbacks with greater emotional resilience. This is the inner gymnasium where transformation takes root.

Now, the Master turns his gaze to the seekers—those burdened by old stories and conditioned fears—and offers a simple, yet radical truth: You are not your past. You are the architect of your future. Through the principles of neuroplasticity, every belief can be rewritten, every identity redefined, and every habit reborn.

In the conversations that follow, you will journey into the heart of mental transformation. With each dialogue, the Master reveals tools and truths to help reshape thought, dissolve fear, and reprogram your mind for breakthrough results. This is not theory—it is practice. It is the art of mental renewal.

And so, the seekers gather in silence, ready to shed the skin of yesterday. For in the sacred work of mental rewiring, they begin to remember: the mind, once awakened, becomes a bridge—leading from limitation to liberation, from habit to higher purpose.

CHAPTER 12

Reprogramming and Rewiring the Brain Through Neuroplasticity

Introduction

You are not bound by your past—your brain is wired to change. The science of neuroplasticity reveals what the sages have always known: with intention and repetition, new patterns can be formed, new beliefs installed, and new realities created. In this illuminating dialogue, the Master teaches the seeker how to break free from old mental scripts and consciously rewire the mind for clarity, confidence, and lasting transformation.

Quote

"Your brain is not a prison of the past—it is the blueprint of your becoming, waiting for your instructions."
—The Master

Dialogue: The Seekers and the Master

Seeker (Caleb): Master, I often feel trapped in old habits. I try to change, but I end up falling back into the same patterns. It feels as if my brain is programmed against me.

Master: That is because it is—your brain has been programmed by repetition, by thoughts rehearsed again until they became automatic.

Caleb: So, am I a prisoner of my past?

Master: Not at all. God designed your brain with something miraculous—neuroplasticity. This means your brain is not fixed. It can rewire itself, form new connections, and release old ones.

Caleb: How do I begin this rewiring?

Master: First, by awareness. Identify the thought patterns and behaviors that no longer serve you. Then replace them with new patterns—thoughts that align with your goals, your values, and God's truth. Each time you repeat the new pattern, your brain carves a stronger pathway.

Caleb: But change feels slow.

Master: Because the old pathways are strong. Think of it as walking through a forest. The old path is wide and well-trodden. The new path is narrow, covered in branches. But the more you walk the new way, the clearer it becomes—while the old path grows over.

Seeker (Darius): Master, I set goals, but my mind drags me into procrastination and doubt. It feels like I am wired to fail.

Master: Darius, what you feel is not weakness—it is wiring. Your brain has built pathways over years of repeated habits. The good news is this: the brain is not fixed. It is plastic—it can change.

Darius: So how do I reprogram my mind to support my goals instead of sabotaging them?

Master: Three practices, Darius:

1. **Affirm and Visualize** – Speak your goal as if it is already true. Picture it vividly. This builds faith and creates new neural connections.

2. **Repeat with Consistency** – Daily practice strengthens the pathway. Just as muscles grow by repetition, so does your brain.
3. **Anchor with Gratitude and Action** – Thank God for progress and take small steps daily. Gratitude reinforces positive wiring; action makes it permanent.

Darius: So, if I speak, visualize, and practice with gratitude and action, I can change my destiny?

Master: Yes. Renew your mind, and you renew your life. As Scripture says, transformation begins within.

Seeker (Malik): Master, can I really change the way I think, feel, and act after so many years of destructive habits?

Master: Malik, the Creator designed your brain with an incredible gift: the power to change. Neuroplasticity is simply the scientific word for what scripture has always taught—that by renewing your mind, you transform your life.

Malik: But the habits feel so deep.

Master: By creating new pathways. Think of your brain like a field. Old habits are deep, worn trails. Neuroplasticity allows you to carve out new trails until they become the main roads. God's Word is the compass that guides you as you rewire those pathways.

Malik: So, I must choose what I focus on?

Master: Exactly. Three practices will accelerate your reprogramming:

1. **Renew Your Mind Daily** – Replace negative thoughts with truth. Use scripture as affirmations, speaking them aloud until they take root.

2. **Visualize the New Path** – Picture yourself acting with discipline, joy, and success. The brain does not distinguish between imagined practice and real practice.
3. **Take Consistent Action** – Small, repeated steps build new habits. Each action reinforces the new pathway until the old one fades.

Malik: And with time, my mind and actions will align with God's design?

Master: Yes, Malik. As you partner with the Spirit and train your mind, you will see transformation in every area of your life.

The Master's Process for Rewiring Your Brain

1. **Identify Old Patterns** – Write down the recurring thoughts or habits that sabotage your progress.
2. **Choose a Replacement** – For each old pattern, create a new thought or action rooted in truth and purpose.
3. **Affirm and Visualize Daily** – Speak the new belief aloud and visualize yourself living it.
4. **Act in Small Steps** – Even small actions repeated daily strengthen the new pathway.
5. **Anchor with Scripture and Gratitude** – Use God's Word and daily thanksgiving to reinforce the new wiring.
6. **Persist Through Resistance** – Remember: old trails are strong. Keep walking the new path until it becomes your default.

Scripture Verse

"Do not conform to the pattern of this world, but be transformed by the renewing of your mind."
– Romans 12:2 (NIV)

"As a man thinketh in his heart, so is he."
– *Proverbs 23:7 (KJV)*

"We take captive every thought to make it obedient to Christ."
– *2 Corinthians 10:5 (NIV)*

Reflective Prayer

Lord of Renewal,
Thank You for the gift of a mind that can be reshaped.
Help me to release destructive patterns and embrace new ones rooted in Your truth.
Grant me persistence to speak life daily,
Vision to see myself as You designed me,
And faith to act even when change feels slow.
Rewire my thoughts, my habits, and my heart,
So that my life may shine with Your transformation.
Amen.

Try This: *21-Day Renewal Practice*

1. **Choose One Old Thought or Habit** – Write it clearly (e.g., "I always procrastinate").
2. **Create a Replacement Statement** – Frame a new truth (e.g., *"I take small steps immediately, and action builds my momentum").*
3. **Affirm Daily** – Speak your replacement statement out loud every morning and evening.
4. **Visualize** – Spend 2–3 minutes picturing yourself living this new truth.
5. **Act Small** – Take one small action each day that proves the new belief.

6. **Track Progress** – Journal daily wins and thank God for each one.

Goal: After 21 days, the old pathway will weaken, and the new one will begin to take root—proving that your brain, with God's guidance, can truly be renewed.

Affirmation to Anchor the Master's Teachings:

"I am rewiring my mind for clarity, confidence, and growth. Each thought I choose creates a new path to the person I am becoming."

CHAPTER 13

Affirmations: Speaking Life into Your Mind and Spirit

Introduction

Words are seeds, and the mind is fertile ground. Whatever you plant consistently will grow. Affirmations are not empty phrases—they are declarations of identity, truth, and intention. When spoken with conviction, they reprogram the subconscious, shift internal dialogue, and redirect your life toward clarity, strength, and purpose. In this transformative conversation, the Master teaches the seeker how to write and speak affirmations that are rooted in truth, charged with emotion, and capable of rewiring the brain for greater personal effectiveness and inner peace.

Quote

"Your words are the brushstrokes of your reality. Speak what you seek, until what you seek begins to speak through you."
—The Master

Dialogue: The Seeker and the Master

Seeker (Samuel): Master, I have heard of affirmations before, but they have always felt a little... forced. Just saying something does not make it true, does it?

Master: Not at first, Samuel. But speak a truth long enough, and your mind begins to believe it. When the mind believes, the body follows. And when the body follows, reality shifts.

Samuel: So, affirmations are more than just positive thinking?

Master: Much more. A true affirmation is a conscious declaration of the reality you are choosing to embody. It is not wishful thinking—it is intentional creation.

Samuel: But how do I make them work for me? I have tried saying things like *"I am successful,"* but it does not always feel real.

Master: That is because effective affirmations must meet four conditions:

1. **They must be present-tense.**
2. **They must be emotionally charged.**
3. **They must be believable—or at least stretch your belief.**
4. **They must be repeated with consistency and conviction.**

Samuel: And what happens when I repeat them?

Master: You create new neural pathways. The brain is designed to respond to repetition. Each time you affirm something with feeling, you weaken the old pattern and strengthen the new one. You are rewiring your identity.

Samuel: And the emotion matters?

Master: Emotion is the glue. If words are the signal, emotion is the amplifier. Say an affirmation with no emotion, and it's like shouting into the wind. But say it with feeling, and the universe listens—and so does your subconscious.

Samuel: How often should I do it?

Master: Morning, evening, and anytime you notice self-doubt creeping in. Use moments of quiet, look yourself in the mirror, speak aloud, and feel the words in your heart. That's how you shift from repeating to becoming.

The Master's Process for Writing and Using Affirmations

1. **Start with Identity** – Begin affirmations with "I am," "I choose," or "I have," affirming your present alignment with the truth you desire.
   Example: "I am disciplined and focused."

2. **Make It Specific and Positive** – Avoid vague language or negative phrasing. Speak clearly and affirm what you *do* want.
   Instead of "I am not afraid," say "I am courageous in the face of fear."

3. **Connect to Emotion** – Include feelings and outcomes that matter. Let the words stir your heart.
   "I feel powerful, peaceful, and prepared."

4. **Repeat with Intention** – Speak them aloud at least twice a day, especially in the morning and before bed. The brain is most impressionable during these times.

5. **Visualize While Speaking** – Imagine the affirmation as already true. Feel it. See it. Experience it in your mind's eye as if it were happening now.

6. **Write Them Down Daily** – Reinforce them through journaling. Writing engages another part of the brain and deepens the neural imprint.

7. **Use Mirror Work** – Look yourself in the eyes while saying your affirmations. It may feel awkward at first, but over time, it builds self-connection and belief.

Scripture Verse

"Death and life are in the power of the tongue, and those who love it will eat its fruit."
—Proverbs 18:21 (NIV)

"Let the weak say, 'I am strong.'"
—Joel 3:10 (NIV)

Reflective Prayer

Creator of Truth and Power,
Teach me to speak life into my soul.
Let my words be aligned with Your promises,
And my thoughts reflect the mind of Christ.
May every declaration I make
Uproot fear, dismantle doubt,
And establish Your truth within me.
Shape my identity with faith-filled words,
And let my spirit grow stronger each day.
Amen.

Try This: *5-Step Affirmation Practice*

1. **Write 3 Core Affirmations** – Begin with "I am," "I have," or "I choose." Focus on areas where you seek growth.
   Examples: "I am confident." "I choose peace." "I have the power to overcome."

2. **Speak Aloud Twice a Day** – Once in the morning and once before sleep, say each affirmation slowly and clearly.

3. **Add Emotion** – As you speak, place your hand on your heart. Feel the truth of the words. Smile. Breathe them in.

4. **Visualize the Outcome** – See yourself living the affirmation. What does it look like? Feel like? Let your imagination support the rewiring process.
5. **Track Your Transformation** – Keep a journal of how you feel each week. Notice shifts in mindset, energy, and behavior.

Goal: To transform your internal dialogue through the power of intentional language, creating new neural pathways that align your mind, body, and spirit with the truth of who you are becoming.

Affirmation to Anchor the Master's Teachings:

"My words have power. I speak life, truth, and possibility into my mind and spirit. What I affirm with faith, I become with time."

Quote

"See it in your mind until your spirit believes it. The clearer the vision, the closer it comes."

—The Master

CHAPTER 14

Visualization: Imprinting the Mind with Possibility

Introduction

What the mind can see, the heart can believe—and what the heart believes, life begins to create. Visualization is not daydreaming. It is mental rehearsal, spiritual alignment, and neural rewiring all at once. In this chapter, the Master reveals how to use the power of imagination and intention to deeply embed affirmations into the subconscious, so they become not just words we speak, but realities we live.

Dialogue: The Seeker and the Master

Seeker (Samuel): Master, I have been saying my affirmations, but some days I feel disconnected—like the words do not stick. Is there more I should be doing?

Master: Yes, Samuel. Speaking plants the seed. But seeing waters it. To truly change your inner world, you must engage your imagination. That is where the imprint begins.

Samuel: You mean, picture it in my mind?

Master: Exactly. Visualization is the art of seeing in the unseen. When you combine your affirmations with mental images—rich in detail, emotion, and energy—you speak to the subconscious in its native language.

Samuel: So, the mind does not just hear the words—it *sees* them?

Master: Yes. The brain does not distinguish between real and vividly imagined experience. What you visualize repeatedly with belief, it accepts as familiar, safe, and true.

Samuel: That is how I rewire the brain?

Master: It is one of the most powerful ways. When you pair a spoken affirmation with a deeply felt visualization, you are creating a mental blueprint. Do it daily, and that blueprint becomes a belief—and beliefs become behavior.

Samuel: How do I know I am doing it right?

Master: Ask yourself: *Can I feel it? Can I see it? Can I believe it—just a little more each time?* The stronger the feeling, the deeper the imprint.

Samuel: And how often should I do this?

Master: Consistency is key. Five to ten minutes in the morning. Five to ten minutes at night. Visualize your affirmation as already true. Smile. Breathe. Feel the gratitude in advance. Then carry that energy into your day.

The Master's Process for Visualization and Imprinting

1. **Find a Quiet Space** – Sit comfortably in a distraction-free zone. Close your eyes and breathe deeply.
2. **Speak Your Affirmation** – Say it aloud or in your mind: *"I am confident." "I choose peace." "I am a vessel of creativity."*
3. **Create a Vivid Image** – Picture yourself living the affirmation. What are you doing? Who are you with? Where are you? Add color, sound, emotion.
4. **Feel It Fully** – Let the feeling rise. Joy. Peace. Confidence. Let it settle in your body as if it is already true.

5. **Anchor the Vision** – Smile. Place your hand on your heart. Breathe deeply. End your visualization with a phrase like, *"It is done."*
6. **Repeat Daily** – Morning and night are the most fertile times for imprinting. Repeat the process consistently to strengthen the neural pathway.

Scripture Verse

"As a man thinketh in his heart, so is he."
—Proverbs 23:7 (KJV)

"Write the vision; make it plain on tablets, so he may run who reads it."
—Habakkuk 2:2 (ESV)

Reflective Prayer

God of Vision and Promise,
Thank You for the power of imagination,
For eyes that see beyond the present moment.
Help me to see what You see in me—
To hold a vision of joy, strength, and purpose.
Let every image I carry align with Your truth,
And let my heart believe before my eyes ever see.
Anchor me in hope,
And train my mind to create with faith.
Amen.

Try This: *5-Step Visualization Practice*

1. **Pick One Affirmation** – Choose an affirmation you want to embody.
   Example: "I am bold and fearless in my calling."

2. **Visualize the Scene** – Close your eyes and see yourself living that truth—walking in confidence, completing a goal, helping others, standing tall.
3. **Engage the Senses** – What do you see, hear, smell, or touch? Engage your senses to strengthen the imprint.
4. **Feel the Emotion** – Let joy, peace, or gratitude rise as if your vision is already real.
5. **Verse the Practice** – Smile. Breathe. Say, "Thank You. It is done." Then step into your day aligned with your vision.

Goal: To embed affirmations into the subconscious by visualizing them as already real — thereby rewiring the brain, reshaping beliefs, and aligning the inner world with the life you are called to live.

Affirmation to Anchor the Master's Teachings:

"I see my future with clarity and conviction. What I visualize with feeling, I move toward with purpose. My mind is aligned with my vision."

CHAPTER 15

Breaking the Chains of Limiting Beliefs

Introduction

The most powerful prisons are the ones we don't know we're in. Limiting beliefs whisper, *You can't... You're not enough... It's too late...* and if left unchallenged, they quietly shape the boundaries of our lives. In this liberating dialogue, the Master guides the seeker to recognize and dismantle these false narratives—replacing them with truths that expand possibility and awaken potential. To break the chains is to remember who you truly are.

Quote

"A limiting belief is just a story you've told yourself too many times. Change the story, and you change your life."
—The Master

Dialogue: The Seekers and the Master

Seeker (Ethan): Master, I keep hearing people say I can do more, achieve more, even become more. But in my heart, I feel stuck. A voice inside says, *"You are not smart enough. You are not worthy. You do not have what it takes."*

Master: That voice, Ethan, is not truth—it is a prison. It is the whisper of limiting beliefs, built over years of wounds, disappointments, and lies you accepted as reality.

Ethan: But Master, these thoughts feel so real. They have been with me for so long. How can I silence them?

Master: You cannot silence them by force, but you can replace them. A lie cannot stand when confronted by truth. To break limiting beliefs, you must:

1. **Identify the Lie** – Name the false belief that has chained you.
2. **Challenge It with Truth** – Ask, *"What does God say about me?"*
3. **Practice New Belief Daily** – Speak affirmations of truth until they become your inner voice.

Ethan: So, it is not about denying my past?

Master: No, Ethan. It is about redefining your future. Your past may explain you, but it does not define you. Remember, the caterpillar does not deny it once crawled; it simply accepts that now it can fly.

Ethan: Then I choose to believe I can fly.

Master: Good. When you exchange the lie for God's truth, you step into the freedom He always intended for you.

Seeker (Nathan): Master, I keep trying to move forward in my life, but something always holds me back. It is not just circumstances—it feels like it is me.

Master: You are correct, Nathan. The greatest prison is not built of stone—it is built of thought.

Nathan: You mean my mind keeps me trapped?

Master: Yes. You are bound by what you believe about yourself. If you believe you are weak, you will never attempt strength. If you believe you are unworthy, you will reject love when it comes.

Nathan: But these beliefs feel so real. They are like truths.

Master: They only feel true because you have repeated them for so long. Every belief is a seed planted in the soil of your heart. If the seed is poison, the fruit will also be poison.

Nathan: Then how do I uproot them?

Master: First, identify the lie. Say it out loud: *"I am not good enough."* Then confront it with truth: *"I am fearfully and wonderfully made."* Replace the poison seed with the seed of life.

Nathan: So, I must speak a new belief?

Master: Yes, for words are powerful. They create the frame for your reality. The world will tell you what you cannot do, but your spirit knows what God placed in you. When your beliefs align with His truth, your chains fall away.

Nathan: And when I feel the old thoughts creeping back?

Master: Do not fight them with fear. Speak again the truth. Over time, the new seed will take root and choke out the old weed. This is how transformation begins.

The Master's Process for Breaking Limiting Beliefs

1. **Identify the Lie** – Write down the specific belief that has held you back.
2. **Challenge with Truth** – Find scripture or affirmations that directly oppose the lie.
3. **Speak Daily** – Declare the new truth every morning and evening.
4. **Visualize Freedom** – Picture yourself living in alignment with the new belief.
5. **Take One Bold Step** – Act in a way that reflects the truth, not the lie. Action strengthens the new pathway.

Scripture Verse

"Do not conform to the pattern of this world but be transformed by the renewing of your mind."
– Romans 12:2 (NIV)

"For as he thinks in his heart, so is he."
– Proverbs 23:7 (KJV)

Reflective Prayer

Heavenly Father,
I lay before You the lies I have believed about myself.
The doubts, the fears, the words spoken over me—
I renounce them in the name of Jesus.
Renew my mind with Your truth.
Let me see myself as You see me:
capable, loved, chosen, and worthy.
Strengthen me daily to walk in this new belief
until my life reflects the freedom You have given me.
Amen.

Try This: *7-Day Belief Reversal Practice*

1. **Day 1 – Write Down One Limiting Belief** (e.g., *"I'm not capable"*).
2. **Day 2 – Find the Truth** – Write a scripture or affirmation that contradicts it - *"I can do all things through Christ who strengthens me"* – Philippians 4:13 (NIV).
3. **Day 3 – Declare It Out Loud** – Speak the truth in the morning and evening.
4. **Day 4 – Visualize** – Spend 2–3 minutes imagining yourself living from the truth.

5. **Day 5 – Act** – Take one action that aligns with the new belief (if you believe you are capable, attempt the task you have been avoiding).
6. **Day 6 – Reflect** – Journal what changed in your emotions, actions, or mindset.
7. **Day 7 – Recommit** – Strengthen the practice for another week, replacing lies with truth until they lose power.

Goal: To uproot the poison of limiting beliefs and plant seeds of truth that align with God's vision for your life.

Affirmation to Anchor the Master's Teachings:

"I release every belief that no longer serves me. I am free to think, believe, and become aligned with my highest truth."

Quote

"Habits shape your results long before your goals do. Master your patterns, and you master your performance."

—The Master

CHAPTER 16

Poor Work Habits: Breaking the Cycle of Inefficiency

Introduction

Success is rarely stolen—it is usually surrendered in small, daily choices. Poor work habits may seem harmless in the moment, but over time, they drain energy, diminish excellence, and erode self-respect. In this practical and revealing dialogue, the Master helps the seeker confront the hidden roots of inefficiency and replace them with rituals of focus, discipline, and flow. True effectiveness begins not in doing more, but in doing what matters—well.

Dialogue: The Seekers and the Master

Seeker (Daniel): Master, I work hard, but somehow, I never feel productive. My desk is always cluttered, my deadlines slip, and I know my habits are holding me back.

Master: Daniel, poor work habits are not a sign of weakness but of misalignment. Your actions do not yet match your intentions. The spirit is willing, but the structure is lacking.

Daniel: So, it is not just about effort?

Master: Effort without order is like pouring water into a cracked vessel. You may work long hours, but much of it seeps away through distraction, disorganization, and lack of focus.

Daniel: That is exactly how it feels. I am exhausted, but my results are small.

Master: The key is discipline disguised as small routines. Order your environment, and your mind will follow. Begin and end each day with clarity—set priorities in the morning, and review progress in the evening. Do not confuse activity with productivity.

Daniel: That is hard for me. I start strong but slip back into old patterns.

Master: Then anchor yourself with accountability. Share your commitments with someone who will ask, *"Did you keep your word?"* Habits are strengthened by repetition, but accountability keeps you from drifting back into chaos.

Daniel: So, the path forward is structure, discipline, and accountability?

Master: Yes, Daniel. When you honor your time, you honor your purpose. Good work habits are not just about efficiency—they are about stewardship of the gifts God has given you.

Seeker (Darius): Master, I find myself trapped in patterns at work that hold me back. I start late, I cut corners, I get distracted, and I rarely finish tasks on time. I know I am capable of better, but these poor habits keep defeating me.

Master: Darius, habits are the silent architects of your life. What you do repeatedly becomes who you are becoming. Poor work habits are not merely about tasks—they erode trust, destroy opportunity, and keep you bound to mediocrity.

Darius: I have tried to change, but I fall back into the same patterns.

Master: That is because you fight the fruit and not the root. Tell me, why do you delay? Why do you cut corners?

Darius: I suppose... I feel overwhelmed. Sometimes I lose motivation. Other times, I do not see the immediate reward for doing things properly.

Master: Then learn this truth: discipline is not about the reward you see today, but about the future it secures tomorrow. Excellence is a habit, not a single act. And trust is built not in great moments, but in small consistent ones.

Darius: How can I rebuild my work habits?

Master: Three practices will set you free:

1. **Structure Your Day** – Set clear times to begin, pause, and finish your tasks.
2. **Focus on One Thing at a Time** – Multitasking scatters the mind, while focus multiplies results.
3. **Finish What You Start** – Completion is a habit. Every unfinished task weakens your spirit.

Darius: And if I fail again?

Master: Then begin again. Each day is a fresh page. Write with discipline, and soon the ink of good habits will replace the stains of poor ones.

The Master's Process for Building Strong Work Habits

1. **Create Structure** – Begin with a clean space and a clear plan each day.
2. **Prioritize** – Decide the top three tasks that matter most before starting work.
3. **Focus Deeply** – Eliminate distractions and give full attention to one task at a time.

4. **Commit to Completion** – Do not abandon a task halfway; discipline grows when you finish.
5. **Review and Reset Daily** – End each day by reviewing what was done, what was missed, and preparing for tomorrow.
6. **Use Accountability** – Share your commitments with someone who can encourage and challenge you.

Scripture Verse

"Whatever you do, work at it with all your heart, as working for the Lord, not for human masters."
– Colossians 3:23 (NIV)

"Let all things be done decently and in order."
– 1 Corinthians 14:40 (KJV)

Reflective Prayer

Heavenly Father,
Deliver me from disorder and waste.
Teach me to honor my time,
To build habits that reflect Your excellence,
And to labor not just with effort, but with wisdom.
May my work be a testimony of diligence and grace,
And may it glorify You in every detail.
Amen.

Try This: *5-Day Work Habit Reset*

1. **Day 1 – Clear Your Space** – Organize your desk or work area before starting. A clean environment creates a clear mind.
2. **Day 2 – Write Your Top 3** – Each morning, list the three most important tasks and do them first.
3. **Day 3 – One Task Rule** – For one day, commit to single-tasking. No multitasking—focus until completion.

4. **Day 4 – Finish Strong** – Before ending the day, complete one task you have been avoiding or leaving half-done.
5. **Day 5 – Reflect and Reset** – Journal what changed in your focus, energy, and productivity. Choose one new habit to carry forward.

Goal: To replace inefficiency with structure, consistency, and accountability—building habits that lead to excellence and trust.

Affirmation to Anchor the Master's Teachings:

"I replace old habits with focused, effective action. I work with clarity, purpose, and intention—turning my time into meaningful results."

Quote

"Your life will always rise—or fall—to the level of your expectations. Set them with intention and live them with integrity."

—The Master

CHAPTER 17

Enhancing Expectations: Raising the Standard of Your Life

Introduction

You do not get what you want—you get what you expect. Expectations act as silent architects, shaping how you think, act, and receive. In this empowering dialogue, the Master teaches the seeker that elevating one's life begins with elevating one's standards. When you expect more from yourself—with clarity, consistency, and courage—you invite life to rise and meet you at the level of your belief.

Dialogue: The Seeker and the Master

Seeker (Jonah): Master, I often feel like I settle for less. Deep down, I want more out of life, but I tell myself not to expect too much—so I will not be disappointed.

Master: Jonah, your life will always rise or fall to the level of your expectations. If you expect little, you will prepare little. If you expect much, you will stretch, grow, and act differently.

Jonah: But if I expect too much, won't I just end up discouraged when things do not work out?

Master: Discouragement does not come from high expectations—it comes from misplaced ones. If your expectations are built on faith, perseverance, and God's truth, they will lift you higher even in struggle. If they are built on fear or entitlement, they will crumble.

Jonah: So, you mean raising my expectations is not just wishing for more?

Master: Correct. It is raising the standard of what you will accept from yourself. Stop expecting mediocrity. Stop telling yourself you are limited. Expect discipline, growth, and excellence. When you expect more of yourself, you begin to demand more from your choices.

Jonah: That feels like a challenge.

Master: It is a holy challenge. God never called you to small thinking. When you align your expectations with His promises, your life will rise to meet them.

The Master's Process for Enhancing Expectations

1. **Examine Your Current Standard** – Ask yourself: *What am I tolerating in my life right now that I know is less than my best?*

2. **Define a Higher Standard** – Write down what "excellent" would look like in your work, relationships, health, and spiritual life.

3. **Speak Faith Over Yourself** – Replace limiting language ("I can't," "I'm not good enough") with truth-filled declarations.

4. **Align Actions with Expectations** – Begin making small, consistent choices that match the higher standard you have set.

5. **Evaluate Regularly** – Each week, ask yourself: *Did my actions reflect the level I now expect of myself?*

Scripture Verse

"According to your faith let it be done to you."
– Matthew 9:29 (NIV)

"Now to him who is able to do immeasurably more than all we ask or imagine, according to his power that is at work within us."
– Ephesians 3:20 (NIV)

Reflective Prayer

Lord of Abundance,
Forgive me for the times I have lowered my expectations out of fear or doubt.
Lift my vision to see myself as You see me—capable, chosen, and called.
Help me to raise the standard of what I expect from my thoughts, words, and actions.
Align my expectations with Your promises,
And give me faith to walk boldly into a greater future.
Amen.

Try This: *The Expectation Upgrade Exercise*

1. Write down **three areas** of your life where you've been settling for less (work, health, relationships, finances, etc.).
2. For each area, write: *What would "excellent" look like if I raised my expectations?*
3. Replace one self-limiting statement with a faith-filled declaration (e.g., *"I'll never get ahead"* → *"God has given me wisdom to prosper."*).

4. Take **one action this week** that reflects the higher expectation (e.g., showing up on time, eating with discipline, preparing fully for a meeting).
5. Journal at week's end: *How did raising my expectations change my behavior and results?*

Goal: To break the cycle of low standards and step into a new level of excellence, built on faith and consistent action.

Affirmation to Anchor the Master's Teachings:

"I elevate my expectations to match my potential. I believe in more, prepare for more, and attract the life I know I am worthy of living."

CHAPTER 18

Expanding the Comfort Zone

Introduction

Growth never happens at the center of comfort. The comfort zone, while familiar and safe, becomes a boundary that quietly limits our dreams. In this courageous conversation, the Master invites the seeker to explore the edge—to embrace uncertainty, stretch into new experiences, and rewire the nervous system to find calm in the unfamiliar. Every time you step beyond what is comfortable, you expand what is possible.

Quote

"Your comfort zone is not your home—it is your starting point. Greatness begins just beyond its edge."
—The Master

Dialogue: The Seeker and the Master

Seeker (David): Master, I find myself living in the same routines. I do what I know, stay where it is safe, and avoid what feels uncertain. But deep down, I feel stuck—as if I am missing out on something greater.

Master: David, comfort is a pleasant prison. It feels safe, but it silently locks the door on your growth. Nothing new grows inside the comfort zone—it is only in the stretch that transformation begins.

David: But Master, when I step outside, I feel fear. My heart races, my thoughts scatter. I want to retreat.

Master: That is natural. Growth always brings discomfort. Think of a muscle—it only grows when stretched and strained. The same is true of your spirit and your potential.

David: So, fear is not a sign that I should stop?

Master: No, David. Fear is the signal that you are moving beyond what you have known. It is the threshold of growth. Courage is not the absence of fear—it is action despite fear.

David: Then how do I expand my comfort zone without becoming overwhelmed?

Master: Step by step. Stretch yourself a little each day. Speak when you would normally stay silent. Try a new skill when you fear failing. Enter new spaces where you feel unqualified. Over time, what was once uncomfortable becomes your new normal.

David: So, my growth is waiting just beyond my fear?

Master: Exactly. Each time you step beyond what is familiar, your comfort zone expands—and with it, your opportunities, your confidence, and your destiny.

The Master's Process for Expanding the Comfort Zone

1. **Identify Your Boundaries** – Write down what feels uncomfortable for you right now (public speaking, networking, taking risks, etc.).
2. **Start Small** – Choose one small action just beyond your current comfort zone.
3. **Lean into Discomfort** – When fear arises, acknowledge it but act anyway.

4. **Reflect on Growth** – After each step, note how your confidence expanded.
5. **Repeat and Build** – Continue stretching little by little. Over time, your new normal will be far greater than your old limits.

Scripture Verse

"Be strong and courageous. Do not be afraid; do not be discouraged, for the Lord your God will be with you wherever you go."
– Joshua 1:9 (NIV)

"For God gave us a spirit not of fear but of power and love and self-control."
– 2 Timothy 1:7 (ESV)

Reflective Prayer

Lord of Courage,
Thank You for being with me in every step I take beyond my comfort.
Help me not to shrink back in fear,
But to step forward in faith.
Stretch my confidence, my skills, and my heart
Until my life reflects the greatness You placed within me.
Give me boldness to embrace the unknown,
And trust that You walk beside me always.
Amen.

Try This: *5-Day Comfort Zone Expansion Challenge*

1. **Day 1 – Name It** – Write down one area of your life where fear holds you back.

2. **Day 2 – Small Step** – Take one small action in that area (speak up in a meeting, start a conversation, try a new approach).
3. **Day 3 – Reflect** – Journal what happened. How did you feel before, during, and after?
4. **Day 4 – Stretch Again** – Take a slightly bigger step in the same area.
5. **Day 5 – Celebrate Growth** – Write down how far you have come and commit to one ongoing stretch each week.

Goal: To prove to yourself that courage grows in the doing—and that your true potential lies just beyond the edges of your comfort zone.

Affirmation to Anchor the Master's Teachings:

"I courageously step beyond what is familiar. Every stretch grows my strength, and every challenge expands what is possible for me."

CHAPTER 19

Eliminating Worry and Overcoming Fear

Introduction

Worry drains the present; fear paralyzes the future. Together, they create an illusion of protection while quietly stealing peace, progress, and power. In this soul-stirring dialogue, the Master helps the seeker unmask fear for what it truly is—a signal, not a sentence—and transform worry into wisdom. To rise above fear is not to feel no fear, but to move forward with trust, courage, and a mind anchored in truth.

Quote

"Fear is a shadow that disappears when you walk toward it with light. Worry is the weight you no longer have to carry."
—The Master

Dialogue: The Seeker and the Master

Seeker (James): Master, I find myself consumed with worry. I worry about money, my family, my work, even the future. The more I worry, the more powerless I feel.

Master: James, worry is a thief. It robs you of peace today without changing tomorrow. Fear is its accomplice—together, they paralyze the heart and cloud the mind.

James: But Master, what if my worries are real? What if my fears come true?

Master: Most of the things you fear will never happen. And even if they do, fear does not prepare you—it weakens you. Faith and action prepare you. Fear imagines defeat before the battle. Faith imagines victory, even in the storm.

James: So how do I let go of worry when it keeps circling in my mind?

Master: You cannot simply let go; you must replace it. Replace worry with prayer. Replace fear with action. Replace doubt with faith. Shift your focus from what you cannot control to what you can.

James: But fear feels so powerful.

Master: That is because you feed it. Whatever you focus on grows. Feed fear with anxious thoughts, and it multiplies. Feed faith with God's promises, and courage rises within you.

James: Then courage is not the absence of fear?

Master: No, James. Courage is faith in motion—choosing to act despite fear. Fear says, *"What if I fail?"* Faith says, *"What if God shows up?"*

The Master's Process for Eliminating Worry and Overcoming Fear

1. **Name Your Fear** – Write down the specific worry or fear that grips you.
2. **Challenge It with Truth** – Ask, *"Is this fear certain—or is it only imagined?"* Replace anxious thoughts with scripture.
3. **Pray Instead of Worry** – Every time the fear arises, turn it into a prayer. Surrender it to God.

4. **Take One Small Action** – Fear loses power when you move forward. Even small steps build courage.
5. **Practice Gratitude** – Fear focuses on lack; gratitude focuses on abundance. Thank God daily for His provision.
6. **Repeat Daily** – Over time, fear weakens, and faith grows strong.

Scripture Verse

"Do not be anxious about anything, but in every situation, by prayer and petition, with thanksgiving, present your requests to God."
– Philippians 4:6 (NIV)

"For God gave us a spirit not of fear but of power and love and self-control."
– 2 Timothy 1:7 (ESV)

"When I am afraid, I put my trust in you."
– Psalm 56:3 (NIV)

Reflective Prayer

Heavenly Father,
I confess that worry and fear have stolen my peace.
Today I lay my anxieties before You.
Replace fear with faith,
Replace worry with trust,
And replace doubt with courage.
Help me to walk in confidence,
Knowing You are with me in every step.
Amen.

Try This: *Fear-to-Faith Journal Practice*

1. **List Your Top 3 Worries** – Write them down honestly.
2. **Rewrite Each as a Prayer** – Turn the worry into a petition (e.g., *"I'm worried about finances" → "Lord, provide wisdom and provision for my finances."*).
3. **Add a Scripture Promise** – Anchor each fear with a verse of truth.
4. **Take One Action** – Do something today, however small, that moves you forward.
5. **End with Gratitude** – Write down 3 blessings that remind you God is already working.

Goal: To shift the mind from paralyzing fear to faithful action, creating a daily rhythm where courage replaces worry.

Affirmation to Anchor the Master's Teachings:

"I release worry and rise above fear. I am grounded in faith, guided by truth, and equipped to face whatever comes my way."

CHAPTER 20

Developing Emotional Resilience: Bouncing Back Stronger

Introduction

Life will test you—not to break you, but to build you. Emotional resilience is the quiet strength that allows you to bend without breaking, to feel deeply without losing direction, and to rise each time with greater wisdom. In this empowering dialogue, the Master teaches the seeker how to turn adversity into alchemy—transforming setbacks into stepping stones and pain into purpose. True strength is not in avoiding a fall, but in learning how to rise.

Quote

"Resilience is not the absence of struggle—it is the decision to rise again, wiser, deeper, and more determined than before."
—The Master

Dialogue: The Seeker and the Master

Seeker (Samuel): Master, life feels like a storm sometimes. I face setbacks at work, conflicts in my relationships, and disappointments that crush my spirit. Each time, it takes me longer to recover. How do I stop being so fragile?

Master: Samuel, you are not fragile—you are untrained. Resilience is not the absence of pain, but the strength to absorb it and rise again. Just as the body builds muscle through resistance, the soul builds strength through trials.

Samuel: But the hits hurt deeply. Sometimes I feel like I cannot take another one.

Master: Pain is real, but it does not define you. What matters is what not happening to you, but what you do with what happens. Will you let it break you, or will you let it shape you?

Samuel: I want to let it shape me, but how?

Master: Three truths will guide you:

1. **Feel, but do not dwell** – Acknowledge your pain, but do not make it your identity.
2. **Reframe the setback** – Ask, *"What can I learn here? How can this make me stronger?"*
3. **Choose your response** – You cannot control the storm, but you can control how you sail through it.

Samuel: So, resilience is not avoiding the blow, but recovering from it?

Master: Exactly. The resilient do not deny the fall—they learn how to rise more quickly. Each recovery builds a stronger spirit, until setbacks become stepping-stones.

The Master's Process for Developing Emotional Resilience

1. **Pause and Breathe** – When struck by a setback, slow down and center yourself.
2. **Name the Pain** – Acknowledge the disappointment, anger, or fear. Hiding it only gives it power.
3. **Reframe the Event** – Ask, *"What is this teaching me? How can I grow from it?"*

4. **Anchor in Faith** – Recall God's promises. Remind yourself that trials are temporary, but His presence is permanent.
5. **Take Small Forward Steps** – Choose one constructive action, however small, that moves you forward.
6. **Practice Recovery Daily** – Build resilience like a muscle—through repetition and intentional practice.

Scripture Verse

"We are hard pressed on every side but not crushed; perplexed, but not in despair; persecuted not abandoned; struck but not destroyed."
– 2 Corinthians 4:8–9 (NIV)

"Though the righteous fall seven times, they rise again."
– Proverbs 24:16 (NIV)

Reflective Prayer

Father of Strength,
Thank You for being my refuge in times of trouble.
When I stumble, lift me.
When I am struck down, renew my spirit.
Teach me not to fear setbacks,
But to see them as opportunities to grow.
Let my heart be steady, my faith unshaken,
And my resilience a testimony of Your power in me.
Amen.

Try This: *5-Step Bounce-Back Exercise*

1. **Identify a Setback** – Think of one recent disappointment or failure.
2. **Write Down the Lesson** – What did this situation teach you about yourself, others, or God?

3. **Choose a New Perspective** – Reframe the event as a stepping-stone rather than a stumbling block.

4. **Take One Positive Step** – Do something small that shows you are moving forward (call a friend, plan the next step, restart the project).

5. **Affirm Daily** – Say aloud: *"I am not defined by my setbacks. I rise stronger each time I fall."*

Goal: To train your spirit to recover faster and stronger, turning every fall into fuel for growth.

Affirmation to Anchor the Master's Teachings:

"I rise each time I fall. Every challenge strengthens me. I am resilient, grounded, and empowered to grow through whatever I go through."

CHAPTER 21

Stress Management: Cultivating Peace Under Pressure

Introduction

Stress is not just what happens to you — it is how you carry what happens. While pressure is a part of life, it does not have to steal your peace. Stress management is the ability to remain grounded in chaos, to respond with clarity under tension, and to protect your inner atmosphere in any environment. In this timely dialogue, the Master teaches the seeker how to breathe through burdens, shift their mindset, and rise with resilience no matter what life brings

Quote

"You may not control the storm, but you can always choose how you anchor your soul within it."
—The Master

Dialogue: The Seeker and the Master

Seeker (Samuel): Master, I feel like I am always on edge. There is so much to do, and so little time. Even when nothing is wrong, my body feels tight—like I am waiting for something to go wrong.

Master: Samuel, you are not broken. You are simply carrying too much without pausing to breathe. Stress is the alarm bell of the soul—it alerts you when something needs attention.

Samuel: But life is stressful! I cannot just walk away from my responsibilities.

Master: Nor should you. But you can change your relationship with pressure. Stress becomes destructive only when we carry it unconsciously. The moment you begin to manage it intentionally; it becomes a tool—not a tyrant.

Samuel: How do I manage it?

Master: Three practices:

1. **Pause and breathe before reacting.**
2. **Speak truth over fear.**
3. **Reframe the pressure as preparation.**
   What presses you can also shape you.

Samuel: And how do I keep a positive attitude when everything feels heavy?

Master: Gratitude is the great stabilizer. Perspective is the great equalizer. When you learn to see beyond the moment, peace finds its way back to you.

The Master's Process for Managing Stress

1. **Anchor in Breath** – Practice deep breathing throughout the day. Inhale peace. Exhale pressure. Even 60 seconds can reset your nervous system.
2. **Name What's True** – Ask, *"Is this pressure real, or am I carrying unnecessary fear?"* Bring awareness to false urgency or perfectionism.
3. **Focus on What You Can Control** – List what is in your power. Release what is not.

4. **Take One Small Step** – Action reduces overwhelm. Choose the next best step. Do not try to fix everything at once.
5. **Schedule Recovery Time** – Build in margin. Step away. Rest is not weakness—it is wisdom.
6. **Speak Life** – Replace anxious thoughts with calm affirmations:
   "I am equipped. I am supported. I can handle this with peace."

Scripture Verse

"Cast all your anxiety on Him because He cares for you."
—1 Peter 5:7 (NIV)

"You will keep in perfect peace those whose minds are steadfast, because they trust in you."
—Isaiah 26:3 (NIV)

Reflective Prayer

God of Peace and Presence,
Still my racing thoughts.
Calm the storms within me.
When pressure builds,
Anchor me in truth.
Help me release what I cannot control,
And act with wisdom in what I can.
Let Your peace rule in my heart,
Even when life feels uncertain.
I trust that You are with me—always.
Amen.

Try This: *5-Day Stress Reset Practice*

1. **Day 1 – Breath Awareness**
   Set a timer 3 times today. Stop everything for 60 seconds and breathe slowly. Inhale for 4, hold for 4, exhale for 4.

2. **Day 2 – Stress Journal**
   Write down what is causing stress. Then list what you can and cannot control. Surrender what is beyond your reach.

3. **Day 3 – Gratitude Shift**
   Name 5 things going right today. Stress shrinks when gratitude expands.

4. **Day 4 – Reframing Practice**
   Choose one stressful situation and reframe it: *"This challenge is building strength in me."*

5. **Day 5 – 10-Minute Joy Break**
   Schedule 10 minutes today to do something life-giving: take a walk, play music, laugh, pray, or rest—no guilt attached.

Goal: To develop the mindset and daily practices that allow you to manage stress with grace, protect your peace under pressure, and build inner resilience through gratitude, breath, and perspective.

Affirmation to Anchor the Master's Teachings:

"I remain calm and centered under pressure. I choose peace over panic and respond to challenges with clarity, strength, and grace."

THE THIRD AREA OF MASTERY
THE SECOND AREA OF MASTERY
THE FIRST AREA OF MASTERY
PART III
MANIFESTATION
Aligning With The Universal Laws

THE THIRD AREA OF MASTERY is learning to live in harmony with the Universal Laws—timeless principles that govern the flow of life itself. When deeply understood and consciously applied, these laws unlock the power to accelerate manifestation, dissolve resistance, and magnetize a life of abundance and wealth.

Mastery of the Universal Laws transforms life from effort to flow. You become one with the divine rhythm of the universe, effortlessly attracting abundance, prosperity, and deep fulfillment. This sacred power has always been within reach—waiting for your soul to remember.

Now, as the journey deepens, the Master turns to a student's eager to understand these sacred principles more intimately. In the quiet space between teacher and seeker, each Universal Law will be revealed—not as abstract theory, but as a living force to be embodied and applied. Through their dialogue, you will discover how these laws operate in the real world, and how you, too, can align with them to create a life of purpose, prosperity, and peace.

And so, the Master invites the seekers to sit beneath the stillness of the stars, where wisdom flows like a quiet river. In the chapters that follow, the sacred laws will be revealed one by one—not as commandments, but as living truths, whispered through the rhythms of the universe. Within the unfolding conversations between Master and students, each law becomes a doorway—guiding the soul toward alignment, illumination, and the graceful art of co-creation.

CHAPTER 22

The First Law: The Law of Vibration

Introduction

In the silence between questions, truth begins to echo. The first sacred law rises like dawn over the horizon of awareness—not to be memorized, but to be felt, lived, and remembered. It is the rhythm beneath all things. It is the hum of the universe.

Quote

"Everything in the universe is in motion. To change your life, you must first learn to change your frequency."
—The Master

Dialogue: The Seeker and the Master

Seeker (Levi): Master, you have spoken of thoughts and attention, but I still don't understand how my inner state truly affects my outer life.

Master: Levi, everything in existence is energy. Your thoughts, your emotions, even your words carry vibration. The Law of Vibration teaches that the frequency you emit attracts experiences that match it.

Levi: So, when I'm filled with fear or anger, I attract more of the same?

Master: Yes. Fear vibrates low and calls more fear to itself. But when you choose love, gratitude, or faith, you raise your vibration—

and you draw to yourself people and circumstances that match those higher states.

Levi: But Master, I can't always control how I feel. Some days I wake heavy with sorrow or anxiety.

Master: That is true, but you can choose practices that lift your frequency. Gratitude, prayer, song, generosity, and laughter—these are instruments that tune your spirit to a higher vibration. The more you practice them, the more natural they become.

Levi: I must learn to live as though my energy is my message to the world?

Master: Exactly, Levi. Your vibration is your broadcast. Ask yourself daily: *"Am I radiating fear, or am I radiating faith?"* The world will respond according to the answer.

The Master's Process for Raising Your Vibration

1. **Guard Your Thoughts** – Replace fear-based thoughts with words of faith and truth.
2. **Practice Gratitude** – Begin and end each day naming blessings, no matter how small.
3. **Engage in Joyful Action** – Sing, laugh, dance, or serve—joy lifts the soul.
4. **Surround Yourself with Light** – Choose uplifting environments, people, and influences.
5. **Connect to Spirit** – Prayer and meditation align your vibration with God's love.

Scripture Verse

"A cheerful heart is good medicine, but a crushed spirit dries up the bones."
– Proverbs 17:22 (NIV)

"Rejoice in the Lord always. I will say it again: Rejoice!"
– Philippians 4:4 (NIV)

Reflective Prayer

Heavenly Father,
Thank You for the gift of life and energy within me.
Teach me to raise my vibration through love, gratitude, and faith.
Help me release fear and resentment,
And fill my heart with joy and peace.
Let my spirit radiate Your light,
So that I may attract experiences that honor Your purpose in me.
Amen.

Try This: *The Vibration Reset Practice*

1. **Morning Tune-Up** – Start the day with prayer and three gratitude statements.
2. **Midday Lift** – When stress rises, pause to breathe deeply and repeat: *"I choose peace, I choose love."*
3. **Evening Joy Ritual** – Do one activity that brings genuine joy (music, walk, laughter, journaling).
4. **Energy Audit** – Ask, *"Did my vibration today reflect faith or fear?"*
5. **Daily Reset** – Each morning, commit again to lift your vibration higher than the day before.

Goal: To consciously raise your frequency through love, joy, gratitude, and faith, attracting experiences that align with your highest self.

Affirmation to Anchor the Master's Teachings:

"I am in harmony with the energy of abundance, peace, and purpose. My thoughts, emotions, and actions vibrate with the frequency of the life I desire."

CHAPTER 23

The Law of Manifestation: Creating with Intention

Introduction

Creation is not a matter of chance—it is the natural result of focused energy and unwavering intention. The Law of Manifestation teaches that what we hold in thought, we begin to shape in form. In this conversation, the Master reveals how to become a conscious creator—no longer drifting through life, but directing it with purpose, clarity, and faith.

Quote

"Manifestation is not magic—it is the art of becoming so aligned with your intention that the universe has no choice but to respond."
—The Master

Dialogue: The Seeker and the Master

Seeker (Elias): Master, you have spoken of attention, gratitude, and vibration. But I still wonder—what is manifestation? People say I can create my reality, but is that truly possible?

Master: Elias, manifestation is not magic. It is alignment. The Law of Manifestation states that everything begins in thought before it becomes reality. When your thoughts, emotions, and actions align with your purpose, you call into being the life God has designed for you.

Elias: So, manifestation is simply about thinking hard enough until something happens?

Master: No, Elias. Thought alone is only the seed. To manifest is to plant that seed with intention, water it with faith and gratitude, and cultivate it with action. Thought begins the process, but belief and action complete it.

Elias: Then what benefit is there for me in mastering manifestation?

Master: The benefit is freedom. When you master manifestation, you stop living only by default—reacting to circumstances—and you begin living by design. You learn to partner with God's creative power. Instead of drifting, you direct. Instead of waiting for change, you become the change.

Elias: That sounds powerful, Master. But what if my manifestations do not come?

Master: Then you must examine your alignment. Are your desires clear, or are they scattered? Are your beliefs empowering, or are they laced with doubt? Are your actions consistent, or only occasional? Manifestation is not about forcing—it is about aligning with the flow of God's plan and your highest intention.

Elias: So, by mastering manifestation, I can live with clarity, purpose, and peace?

Master: Yes. For the one who manifests with wisdom is not chasing life—he is co-creating it.

The Master's Process for Manifestation

1. **Set a Desirable Goal** – Be specific about what you truly want.

2. **Make It a SMART Goal** – Specific, Measurable, Attainable, Relevant, Time-bound.
3. **Create a Plan** – Break the goal into steps; commit them to writing.
4. **Work the Plan** – Time-block your calendar and honor the commitments.
5. **Check and Adjust** – Review your results, refine your actions, and repeat until success comes.
6. **Anchor With Faith and Gratitude** – Thank God daily for progress and for what is already on the way.

Scripture Verse

"Write the vision; make it plain on tablets, so he may run who reads it."
– Habakkuk 2:2 (ESV)

"As a man thinketh in his heart, so is he."
– Proverbs 23:7 (KJV)

Reflective Prayer

Creator God,
Thank You for the gift of imagination,
And for the power to bring vision into reality.
Help me to align my thoughts with Your truth,
My emotions with Your peace,
And my actions with Your purpose.
Teach me to plant with faith,
To water with gratitude,
And to harvest in Your perfect timing.
Amen.

Try This: *The Manifestation Alignment Practice*

1. **Daily Vision** – Spend 5 minutes visualizing your goal as if it is already complete.
2. **SMART Check** – Rewrite your goal as a SMART statement and review it weekly.
3. **Time Block** – Dedicate at least one daily block of time to work toward it.
4. **Gratitude Anchor** – Speak three things you are grateful for related to this goal.
5. **Faith Declaration** – End the day with this affirmation: *"What I focus on with faith, gratitude, and action is already on its way."*

Goal: To shift from passive wishing to active creation—aligning thought, belief, and action so that your life unfolds with purpose and abundance.

Affirmation to Anchor the Master's Teachings:

"I manifest my desires through clear intention, focused action, and unwavering faith. What I create begins within me and flows into my reality."

CHAPTER 24

The Law of Creation: Thoughts Become Reality

Introduction

Every thought is a seed, and the mind is sacred ground. The Law of Creation reveals that reality is not something we merely encounter—it is something we continually shape from within. In this dialogue, the Master guides the seekers to understand that thoughts are not idle—they are instruments of creation, shaping the outer world in the image of the inner one.

Quote

"Your world is born first in the unseen—crafted by thought, sculpted by belief, and made real by the energy you give it."
—The Master

Dialogue: The Seeker and the Master

Seeker (Elias): Master, I have often wondered—how do people create lives of abundance, opportunity, or success, while others remain stuck in lack?

Master: Elias, all creation begins first in thought. Every invention, every building, every song, every dream fulfilled—each one was first imagined before it became reality. You are always creating—whether consciously or unconsciously.

Elias: So, my life today is the result of the thoughts I held yesterday?

Master: Exactly. Your dominant thoughts shape your choices, your choices shape your actions, and your actions shape your destiny. What you dwell upon expands. You are a co-creator with God and with the universe itself.

Elias: But what if my thoughts are full of fear and doubt?

Master: Then fear and doubt will shape your reality. But you can choose differently. By aligning your thoughts with truth, gratitude, and faith, you call into being the life God has designed for you.

Elias: So, creation is not just about wishing—it is about aligning my thoughts and actions?

Master: Correct. Faith without works is dead. Thoughts are the seeds, but action waters them. When your thoughts, words, and deeds are aligned, the harvest will come.

The Master's Process for the Law of Creation

1. **Clarify Your Vision** – Write down clearly what you desire to create. Be specific.
2. **Focus Your Thoughts** – Daily, imagine the outcome as though it already exists.
3. **Speak It Aloud** – Words carry creative power. Speak life, not defeat.
4. **Take Inspired Action** – Do what is in your power today that moves you closer to your vision.
5. **Trust the Process** – Release the "how" to God. Stay persistent and faithful.

Scripture Verse

"As a man thinketh in his heart, so is he."
– Proverbs 23:7 (KJV)

"Now faith is confidence in what we hope for and assurance about what we do not see."
– Hebrews 11:1 (NIV)

Reflective Prayer

Creator of Heaven and Earth,
Thank You for giving me the power to shape my life through thought, word, and action.
Help me to align my mind with Your truth,
My heart with Your will,
And my steps with Your purpose.
May my thoughts be seeds of faith,
My words carry life,
And my actions bring forth the harvest You have prepared.
Amen.

Try This: *The 7-Day Creation Practice*

1. **Day 1 – Write a Vision** – Choose one goal or desire and write it as if it is already real.
2. **Day 2 – Visualize** – Spend 5 minutes picturing this reality in vivid detail.
3. **Day 3 – Speak It** – Create one affirmation aligned with your vision. Say it daily.
4. **Day 4 – Take a Step** – Do one small action that moves you toward your vision.
5. **Day 5 – Gratitude Journal** – Write 3 things daily that align with your desired outcome.

6. **Day 6 – Release** – In prayer, give the "how" to God. Trust the unfolding.
7. **Day 7 – Review** – Reflect on what shifted in your energy, focus, and results.

Goal: To train your mind and spirit to consciously create in partnership with God, rather than unconsciously drift into fear or doubt.

Affirmation to Anchor the Master's Teachings:

"My thoughts are powerful and creative. I choose to think with intention, believe with faith, and shape my reality through the truth I hold in mind."

CHAPTER 25

The Law of Attraction: Drawing What You Project

Introduction

The universe is a mirror, reflecting not what you desire, but what you are. The Law of Attraction teaches that we do not chase what we seek—we attract it by the frequency we emit. In this sacred exchange, the Master reveals how to become a living magnet, drawing people, opportunities, and experiences that resonate with your inner truth.

Quote

"What you project into the world returns to you dressed in form—your energy is the invitation, your belief the blueprint."
—The Master

Dialogue: The Seeker and the Master

Seeker (Noah): Master, I keep noticing a pattern. When I am anxious, more problems seem to come. When I am hopeful, opportunities appear. Is it just coincidence?

Master: No, Noah. You are experiencing the Law of Attraction. You draw into your life the people, circumstances, and opportunities that align with the energy you project.

Noah: So, you are saying my inner state shapes what shows up around me?

Master: Exactly. Your thoughts, feelings, and words are signals you send into the universe. Like a magnet, you attract what resonates with your vibration. Fear attracts more fear. Faith attracts more faith. Gratitude attracts more blessings.

Noah: But Master, what if I try to think positively, yet my situation remains the same?

Master: The Law of Attraction is not about wishing—it is about alignment. If your thoughts say one thing, but your actions say another, the signal is broken. You must align your beliefs, your words, and your deeds. Then creation responds.

Noah: So, it is more than positive thinking?

Master: Much more. It is purposeful living. It is faith in motion. When your mind focuses on what you desire, your heart believes it possible, and your actions demonstrate commitment, then opportunities are drawn to you as surely as the tide follows the moon.

Noah: Then I am not a victim of chance, but a participant in creation?

Master: Yes, Noah. You are a co-creator with God. The energy you project is the invitation you send into the world.

The Master's Process for Activating the Law of Attraction

1. **Clarify What You Desire** – Be specific. Vague intentions create vague results.
2. **Align Your Thoughts and Emotions** – See yourself already living it. Feel the joy, gratitude, and confidence as though it is real now.
3. **Speak Life** – Use affirmations rooted in faith, not fear. Speak what you desire, not what you dread.

4. **Take Inspired Action** – Move daily in the direction of your desire. Action shows the universe—and God—that you are ready.
5. **Release and Trust** – Do not obsess or cling in worry. Surrender the timing to God's wisdom, while remaining faithful in your efforts.

Scripture Verse

"As a man thinketh in his heart, so is he."
– Proverbs 23:7 (KJV)

"According to your faith be it unto you."
– Matthew 9:29 (KJV)

"You will also decree a thing, and it will be established for you; and light will shine on your ways."
– Job 22:28 (NASB)

Reflective Prayer

Heavenly Father,
Thank You for the power of thought, word, and faith.
Teach me to align my heart with Your truth,
My words with Your promises,
And my actions with Your calling.
Let me attract what is good,
Release what is harmful,
And walk in harmony with the life You designed for me.
Amen.

Try This: *The Attraction Alignment Practice*

1. **Write Your Desire** – One clear statement of what you want to draw into your life.

2. **Visualize Daily** – Spend 5 minutes imagining it already real. Feel the emotions of gratitude and joy.
3. **Create an Affirmation** – Speak it aloud every morning (e.g., *"I am walking in abundance and purpose."*).
4. **Take One Step** – Each day, do something that aligns with your desire.
5. **Gratitude Review** – Each evening, write down 3 ways you already see God's hand at work.

Goal: To live in alignment—where thoughts, feelings, and actions project faith and expectancy, drawing opportunities, people, and blessings into your life.

Affirmation to Anchor the Master's Teachings:

"I attract what I radiate. As I align my thoughts, emotions, and energy with love, abundance, and purpose, I draw those very things into my life."

CHAPTER 26

The Law of Attention: What You Focus On Expands

Introduction

Where your attention goes, energy flows—and reality follows. The Law of Attention reveals that focus is not a passive act, but a creative force. In this teaching, the Master shows the seekers how to discipline the mind, clear distractions, and place awareness on what truly matters. For whatever you nourish with your gaze, grows.

Quote

"The universe responds to the direction of your focus. What you water with attention will rise and take root in your life."
—The Master

Dialogue: The Seeker and the Master

Seeker (Micah): Master, I notice my mind often drifts to my problems—debts, failures, worries. The more I think about them, the heavier they feel, and the more they seem to grow.

Master: Micah, you have discovered the Law of Attention. Whatever you consistently focus on expands. Focus on problems, and they multiply. Focus on possibilities, and they increase.

Micah: But how can my attention have so much power?

Master: Because attention is energy. Wherever you place it, you feed. Just as sunlight makes a plant grow, your focus makes circumstances stronger in your life.

Micah: Then am I doomed if my mind keeps going to the negative?

Master: Not doomed, but undisciplined. The mind is like a wild horse—it runs where it pleases until you train it. Attention must be directed with intention.

Micah: How do I do that?

Master: By practicing three steps:

1. **Awareness** – Notice where your focus goes.
2. **Redirect** – When you catch yourself feeding fear or negativity, shift your attention to faith, gratitude, or solutions.
3. **Repetition** – The more you practice, the stronger your focus becomes.

Micah: So, attention is not passive—it is a choice?

Master: Exactly. Each day, you decide where to shine the light of your attention. And that choice shapes the quality of your experiences

The Master's Process for Mastering the Law of Attention

1. **Audit Your Attention** – Write down what occupies most of your thoughts daily.
2. **Identify Energy Drains** – Note the negative focus points that weaken your spirit.
3. **Choose a Worthy Focus** – Decide what is worthy of your attention (faith, growth, purpose, solutions).
4. **Create Daily Rituals** – Begin and end your day focusing on gratitude, scripture, and affirmations.

5. **Redirect in the Moment** – When negativity pulls you in, pause, breathe, and consciously shift your focus to what you desire.

Scripture Verse

"You keep him in perfect peace whose mind is stayed on you, because he trusts in you."
– Isaiah 26:3 (ESV)

"Finally, brothers and sisters, whatever is true, whatever is noble, whatever is right, whatever is pure, whatever is lovely, whatever is admirable—if anything is excellent or praiseworthy—think about such things."
– Philippians 4:8 (NIV)

Reflective Prayer

Lord of Light,
Teach me to guard my attention,
To focus not on fear or lack,
But on Your truth, Your promises, and Your goodness.
Help me to redirect my thoughts when they wander,
To dwell on what builds life and peace,
And to keep my mind aligned with Your will.
Amen.

Try This: *3-Point Focus Reset*

1. **Morning Focus** – Write down three things you will focus on today that align with your goals and faith.
2. **Midday Check-In** – Pause midday and ask: *"Where is my attention right now? Am I feeding faith or fear?"* Redirect as needed.

3. **Evening Gratitude** – Before bed, write down three moments where shifting your focus changed your outlook or results.

Goal: To train your mind daily to focus on what multiplies life and peace, so you expand what truly matters.

Affirmation to Anchor the Master's Teachings:

"My thoughts shape my world. I choose thoughts of faith, purpose, and possibility, knowing they create the reality I am destined to live."

CHAPTER 27

The Law of Acceptance: Finding Peace in What Is

Introduction

To resist what is, is to suffer. The Law of Acceptance invites the seeker to release the inner struggle and meet life with open arms. In this gentle yet profound teaching, the Master reminds us that peace does not come from changing the world, but from changing our relationship to it. Acceptance is not surrender—it is alignment with the present moment, where clarity, strength, and freedom reside.

Quote

"Acceptance is not giving up—it is waking up to the wisdom hidden within what is."
—The Master

Dialogue: The Seeker and the Master

Seeker (Aaron): Master, I spend so much of my time wishing things were different — wishing I had more money, wishing my relationships were better, wishing my past mistakes never happened. The weight of it all makes me restless.

Master: Aaron, peace begins when you stop wrestling with what is. Resistance to reality breeds suffering. Acceptance is not surrender to defeat—it is alignment with truth.

Aaron: But Master, if I accept things as they are, won't I stop striving to improve them?

Master: No. Acceptance does not mean passivity. It means acknowledging the truth of this moment, without denial or bitterness. From there, you gain the clarity and strength to act wisely. You cannot change what you refuse to face.

Aaron: So, my struggle is not with life itself, but with my refusal to embrace it as it is?

Master: Exactly. The river flows whether you fight it or not. Resistance exhausts you; acceptance allows you to steer with the current. True power comes not from denying reality, but from accepting it and choosing your response.

Aaron: That feels freeing, but difficult.

Master: Difficult at first, yes. But remember—every moment of life, even the painful ones, can be your teacher if you accept it. In acceptance, you find peace. In peace, you find wisdom. And in wisdom, you find the next step forward.

The Master's Process for Practicing the Law of Acceptance

1. **Name What Is** – Acknowledge the reality of your current situation without excuses or denial.
2. **Release Resistance** – Notice where you are fighting life with "shoulds" and "if onlys." Let them go.
3. **Shift Perspective** – Ask: *What lesson or gift could this moment hold for me?*
4. **Choose Peace** – Replace frustration with gratitude for what is still good.
5. **Act from Clarity** – Once you accept reality, choose the wisest next step without fear or resentment.

Scripture Verse

"Be still, and know that I am God."
– Psalm 46:10 (NIV)

"For I have learned to be content whatever the circumstances."
– Philippians 4:11 (NIV)

Reflective Prayer

Lord of Peace,
I confess that I have resisted life as You have allowed it.
I have fought against what is,
And in doing so, I have lost my peace.
Teach me to accept the present moment,
To find wisdom in what I cannot change,
And to act with faith in what I can.
Let Your peace guard my heart and mind,
As I trust in You fully.
Amen.

Try This: *The Daily Acceptance Practice*

1. **Morning Reflection** – Begin the day by writing one thing you struggle to accept.
2. **Reframe It** – Ask yourself: *If I accept this as it is today, what peace can I find?*
3. **Affirm It** – Speak aloud: *"I accept this moment as my teacher. I will learn and grow from it."*
4. **Evening Gratitude** – End the day by writing three blessings that came from simply accepting life as it unfolded.
5. **Repeat Daily** – Over time, acceptance will replace resistance, and peace will become your natural posture.

Goal: To cultivate peace by embracing life as it is, while gaining the clarity and strength to act wisely for the future.

Affirmation to Anchor the Master's Teachings:

"I release resistance and accept this moment with peace. I trust that everything is unfolding for my highest good, even when I don't yet understand it."

CHAPTER 28

The Law of Forgiveness: Releasing to Be Free

Introduction

Forgiveness is the key that unlocks the chains of the past. The Law of Forgiveness teaches that holding onto pain binds you to what was, while release sets you free to become what can be. In this tender exchange, the Master guides the seekers through the sacred art of letting go—not to excuse, but to unburden the soul and make space for healing, compassion, and renewal.

Quote

"Forgiveness is not about others—it is the gift you give yourself to reclaim your peace and remember your wholeness."
—The Master

Dialogue: The Seeker and the Master

Seeker (Jonah): Master, I carry wounds from my past. People have wronged me, betrayed me, and hurt me deeply. I tell myself I have moved on, but inside, I still burn with resentment.

Master: Jonah, resentment is a chain that binds the soul. It ties you to the very pain you wish to escape. Forgiveness is the key that breaks that chain—not for them, but for you.

Jonah: But Master, if I forgive, doesn't that mean I excuse what they did?

Master: No, forgiveness does not erase the wrong. It simply releases your spirit from carrying the weight of it. You cannot heal while clutching the wound. Forgiveness is not approval—it is freedom.

Jonah: But what if the person never apologizes?

Master: Forgiveness is not dependent on their repentance. It is a choice you make for your own soul. To wait for their apology is to remain imprisoned. To forgive is to walk free, regardless of what they do.

Jonah: And what if I cannot forgive myself? My own mistakes haunt me.

Master: Then you must remember—God has already offered you grace. If the Creator has forgiven you, who are you to withhold it from yourself? Self-forgiveness is an act of humility and faith.

The Master's Process for Practicing Forgiveness

1. **Acknowledge the Wound** – Be honest about the hurt. Naming it begins the healing.
2. **Release the Burden** – Decide to let go, not for them, but for your own freedom.
3. **Pray for the Offender** – This does not excuse them but releases bitterness from your heart.
4. **Forgive Yourself** – Write down mistakes you have held against yourself, then declare God's forgiveness over them.
5. **Choose Freedom Daily** – Forgiveness is often a process. Each time resentment rises, release it again until peace comes.

Scripture Verse

"Bear with each other and forgive one another if any of you has a grievance against someone. Forgive as the Lord forgave you."
– Colossians 3:13 (NIV)

"For if you forgive other people when they sin against you, your heavenly Father will also forgive you."
– Matthew 6:14 (NIV)

Reflective Prayer

Merciful Father,
I bring before You the wounds I have carried.
I release resentment, bitterness, and pain into Your hands.
Teach me to forgive as You have forgiven me.
Grant me the grace to forgive others,
The humility to forgive myself,
And the courage to walk in freedom.
Let my heart be healed,
And my spirit made whole through Your love.
Amen.

Try This: *The Forgiveness Release Exercise*

1. **List the Weights** – Write down the names of people (including yourself) you still hold resentment against.
2. **Speak Release** – One by one, say aloud: *"I forgive you. I release you. I choose peace."*
3. **Pray Over the List** – Ask God to fill the space once held by bitterness with His love.
4. **Tear and Discard** – Destroy the paper as a symbolic act of release.

5. **Practice Daily** – Each time resentment rises, repeat the words: *"I forgive. I release. I am free."*

Goal: To clear the heart of resentment so that healing and growth can take root in the space forgiveness creates.

Affirmation to Anchor the Master's Teachings:

"I forgive fully and release the weight of the past. In forgiveness, I set myself free and open my heart to healing and peace."

CHAPTER 29

The Law of Allowing: Living in Harmony Without Judgment

Introduction

True freedom is born in the space where judgment ends. The Law of Allowing teaches the seeker to release the need to control, fix, or condemn—and instead, to honor the sacred path of every soul, including their own. In this quiet teaching, the Master reveals the wisdom of non-resistance, the strength of compassion, and the grace that flows when we live in harmony with what is, without needing to make it right or wrong.

Quote

"Allowing is not weakness—it is the highest form of strength: the power to let life unfold without needing to make it yours."
—The Master

Dialogue: The Seeker and the Master

Seeker (Eli): Master, I find myself frustrated with people. I want them to think like me, act like me, and live the way I believe is right. When they do not, I get angry or disappointed.

Master: Eli, what you describe is resistance—the belief that others must live according to your script. But harmony is found not in control, but in allowing. The Law of Allowing teaches that love gives freedom, not chains.

Eli: But if I allow people to live as they want, what if they make mistakes?

Master: Mistakes are the teachers of life. Just as you have learned through your own, they must learn through theirs. To demand perfection from others is to forget your own humanity.

Eli: So, the Law of Allowing means I should just accept everything?

Master: Acceptance does not mean agreement. It means choosing not to judge or control. You can disagree without dishonoring. You can correct without condemning. Allowing means holding space for others to walk their path, while you remain faithful to yours.

Eli: That feels difficult—my instinct is to fix, to correct, to change others.

Master: The need to control comes from fear. But love allows. Love trusts that God is working in others just as He works in you. The Law of Allowing keeps you aligned with peace, because you stop fighting battles that were never yours to fight.

The Master's Process for Practicing the Law of Allowing

1. **Release Control** – Remind yourself: *I cannot live another's life for them.*
2. **Choose Compassion** – See others as learners on their journey, not enemies to be corrected.
3. **Detach from Judgment** – Replace "They should…" with "I allow them to…"
4. **Focus on Your Path** – Direct your energy to living your truth fully.

5. **Trust God's Timing** – Believe that He is working in their hearts as He is in yours.

Scripture Verse

"Do not judge, or you too will be judged."
– Matthew 7:1 (NIV)

"Accept the one whose faith is weak, without quarreling over disputable matters."
– Romans 14:1 (NIV)

Reflective Prayer

Lord of Mercy,
Teach me to release my need to control others.
Help me to walk in love, not judgment,
To honor each person's journey,
And to trust that You are at work in all of us.
Grant me peace where I cannot change,
Patience where I am tempted to control,
And compassion in every interaction.
Amen.

Try This: *The Allowing Practice*

1. **Notice the Urge to Control** – When you feel frustration with someone's choices, pause and name it.
2. **Shift the Language** – Instead of saying, *"They should do this,"* say, *"I allow them their journey."*
3. **Practice Compassion** – Write down one positive quality about the person you are tempted to judge.
4. **Refocus on You** – Ask, *"What can I control in my own life right now?"*

5. **Daily Reflection** – Each evening, note one moment where you chose allowing instead of judging, and how it shifted your peace.

Goal: To release unnecessary control and judgment, and to create space for love, peace, and harmony in relationships.

Affirmation to Anchor the Master's Teachings:

"I forgive fully and release the weight of the past. In forgiveness, I set myself free and open my heart to healing and peace."

CHAPTER 30

The Law of Detachment: Freedom Through Trust

Introduction

Detachment is not indifference—it is sacred trust in the unfolding of life. The Law of Detachment invites the seeker to release the grip of control and lean into the unknown with faith. In this profound lesson, the Master teaches that freedom arises when we let go of outcomes, surrender timelines, and trust the intelligence of the universe to bring forth what serves our highest good.

Quote

"Detachment is not about walking away—it is about walking free, anchored in trust that what is meant for you will never miss you."
—The Master

Dialogue: The Seeker and the Master

Seeker (Lucas): Master, I find myself clinging to outcomes. I pray for success, but I constantly worry about how and when it will happen. I try to control every detail, but the more I grasp, the more frustrated I become.

Master: Lucas, you have mistaken control for security. True freedom does not come from holding tighter, but from letting go. The Law of Detachment teaches that peace is found when you release the need to control outcomes and trust the greater plan.

Lucas: But if I do not hold on, won't I lose what I want?

Master: No. Detachment is not indifference. It is trust. It means you set your intention, take faithful action, and then release the timing and the form of the result. When you cling, you create fear. When you trust, you create flow.

Lucas: So, I should still pursue my goals, but without obsession?

Master: Exactly. Pursue with diligence, but hold with open hands. When you are detached, you live with peace in the present moment, while still moving toward the future.

Lucas: But what if things do not turn out as I hoped?

Master: Then you will discover they turned out as they needed. Detachment allows you to rest in the truth that God's plan is wiser than yours. What is meant for you will not pass you by.

The Master's Process for Practicing Detachment

1. **Set Your Intention** – Be clear about what you desire and align it with your highest values.
2. **Take Faithful Action** – Do what you can each day to move toward it.
3. **Release the Outcome** – Stop obsessing over when and how it must happen.
4. **Trust the Timing** – Believe that God's plan and timing are greater than your own.
5. **Stay Present** – Live fully in the now, knowing the future is unfolding as it should.

Scripture Verse

"Cast all your anxiety on him because he cares for you."
– 1 Peter 5:7 (NIV)

"Trust in the Lord with all your heart and lean not on your own understanding; in all your ways submit to him, and he will make your paths straight."
– Proverbs 3:5–6 (NIV)

Reflective Prayer

Heavenly Father,
I release my grip on outcomes I cannot control.
Teach me to trust Your wisdom,
To set my intentions with faith,
And to take action without fear.
Calm my anxious heart,
And help me live with open hands,
Believing that what is meant for me
Will come in Your perfect timing.
Amen.

Try This: *The Open Hands Practice*

1. **Name Your Attachment** – Write down one outcome you are clinging to (a job, relationship, success).
2. **Set Your Intention** – Write what you desire clearly and faithfully.
3. **Take One Step** – Do one action today that moves you closer to it.
4. **Release It in Prayer** – Hold your written intention in your hands, then physically open your hands, and say, *"I release this to God."*

5. **Live in Trust** – Each time anxiety rises, repeat aloud: *"What is meant for me will not pass me by."*

Goal: To experience peace by trusting the divine flow, instead of being chained to fear or control.

Affirmation to Anchor the Master's Teachings:

"I let go of control and trust the divine timing of my life. I release outcomes and walk in peace, knowing what is meant for me will find me."

CHAPTER 31

The Law of Gratitude: Multiplying Blessings

Introduction

Gratitude is the amplifier of all that is good. The Law of Gratitude reminds us that what we appreciate, appreciates. In this radiant teaching, the Master reveals how thankfulness shifts perception, expands possibility, and multiplies the blessings already present. Gratitude is not merely a feeling—it is a frequency that tunes the soul to abundance, joy, and the quiet miracle of now.

Quote

"Gratitude turns what you have into more than enough—it is the secret door through which abundance flows."
—The Master

Dialogue: The Seeker and the Master

Seeker (David): Master, I often pray for more—more opportunities, more success, more joy. But sometimes, I feel like my prayers go unanswered.

Master: David, blessings do not multiply by asking alone—they multiply through gratitude. The Law of Gratitude says: *What you appreciate expands.*

David: But Master, how can being thankful bring me more?

Master: Gratitude is the language of abundance. When you give thanks, you acknowledge the good already present in your life, and you open the door for more. A thankful heart tells God, *"I see Your* *hand at work."* That awareness shifts your spirit and attracts increase.

David: But what about when life feels heavy? When there does not seem to be much to be grateful for?

Master: That is when gratitude is most powerful. Gratitude in plenty is appreciation. Gratitude in lack is faith. When you give thanks even in the storm, you anchor yourself in hope, and you draw strength to endure and rise again.

David: So, gratitude is not just a feeling—it is a practice?

Master: Exactly. It is a discipline of the heart. The grateful man sees blessings where others see burdens. And because he sees them, more blessings come.

The Master's Process for Practicing the Law of Gratitude

1. **Notice the Good** – Each day, list at least three blessings, no matter how small.
2. **Express Thanks Aloud** – Speak your gratitude, for words shape your spirit.
3. **Turn Trials into Teachers** – Ask, *"What hidden gift does this challenge carry?"*
4. **Show Appreciation to Others** – Gratitude shared multiplies in both giver and receiver.
5. **Make Gratitude a Lifestyle** – Begin and end every day with thanksgiving.

Scripture Verse

"Give thanks in all circumstances; for this is God's will for you in Christ Jesus."
– 1 Thessalonians 5:18 (NIV)

"Enter his gates with thanksgiving and his courts with praise; give thanks to him and praise his name."
– Psalm 100:4 (NIV)

Reflective Prayer

Heavenly Father,
Thank You for the blessings I often overlook.
Thank You for the breath in my lungs,
For the people I love,
For the opportunities before me.
Teach me to give thanks in all things,
Not only when life is easy,
But when trials come,
That my heart may remain anchored in Your goodness.
May gratitude open my eyes to see more of You
And multiply blessings in my life.
Amen.

Try This: *The Gratitude Log*

1. **Morning Gratitude** – Write down three things you are thankful for as soon as you wake up.
2. **Gratitude Breaks** – Pause twice during the day and give thanks for something happening in the moment.
3. **Evening Reflection** – Before bed, record three blessings that came during the day.

4. **Weekly Gratitude Letter** – Once a week, write (and send, if possible) a note of thanks to someone in your life.
5. **Gratitude Reframe** – When faced with a challenge, write one thing about it you can still be thankful for.

Goal: To train your mind and heart to see blessings everywhere, multiplying joy, peace, and opportunities.

Affirmation to Anchor the Master's Teachings:

"I live with a grateful heart. Every moment, every breath, every blessing multiplies as I give thanks for all I have and all that is on its way."

CHAPTER 32

The Law of Giving: Abundance Flows Through Generosity

Introduction

To give is to open the channel through which abundance flows. The Law of Giving teaches that generosity is not about what you lose, but what you activate. In this powerful teaching, the Master guides the seekers to understand that true giving comes from the heart—not out of obligation, but from overflow. When you give freely, without fear or expectation, you enter the divine circulation of life, where blessings move through you and return magnified.

Quote

"What you give from love never leaves you — it flows forward, multiplies, and finds its way back in unexpected and beautiful forms."
—The Master

Dialogue: The Seeker and the Master

Seeker (Samuel): Master, I have worked hard to build a stable life, but I fear letting go of what I have earned. I hold tightly to my money, my time, even my talents. Yet despite all my efforts, abundance seems far away.

Master: Samuel, the universe does not reward closed fists. The Law of Giving teaches that abundance flows through generosity. What you hold too tightly withers, but what you release multiplies.

Samuel: But Master, if I give, won't I have less?

Master: No, Samuel. Giving is not subtraction—it is circulation. Just as rivers stay alive by flowing, so does abundance flow when you give freely. When you release with love, life returns it to you in unexpected ways.

Samuel: But what if I have little to give?

Master: Then give from where you are. A smile, an encouraging word, a small act of kindness—these are treasures, too. What matters is not the size of the gift, but the spirit in which it is given.

Samuel: So, giving is not just about money?

Master: Exactly. You can give time, compassion, wisdom, forgiveness, and service. The universe and God respond to the intention of the heart. When you give with joy, you create space for abundance to flow back to you.

The Master's Process for Practicing the Law of Giving

1. **Give Intentionally** – Choose each day to give something—whether time, talent, or treasure.
2. **Give Freely** – Release without expecting anything in return. Trust the flow of life.
3. **Give Joyfully** – Let giving come from love, not guilt or obligation.
4. **Give Creatively** – Look for ways beyond money: encouragement, mentorship, presence.
5. **Receive Graciously** – Allow others to give to you as well. Abundance flows in both directions.

Scripture Verse

"Give, and it will be given to you. A good measure, pressed down, shaken together and running over, will be poured into your lap. For

with the measure you use, it will be measured to you."
– Luke 6:38 (NIV)

"The generous will themselves be blessed, for they share their food with the poor."
– Proverbs 22:9 (NIV)

Reflective Prayer

Lord of Abundance,
Teach me to live with open hands.
Remove fear from my giving,
And fill me with joy to bless others.
Help me to see that generosity is not loss,
But the pathway to multiplication.
As I give, let my heart reflect Your own,
And may my life become a channel of Your love and provision.
Amen.

Try This: *The 7-Day Giving Challenge*

1. **Day 1 – Give Encouragement** – Speak life into someone who is struggling.
2. **Day 2 – Give Time** – Dedicate an hour to help another without expecting reward.
3. **Day 3 – Give Resources** – Share a book, meal, or money with someone in need.
4. **Day 4 – Give Gratitude** – Write a heartfelt thank-you to someone who impacted your life.
5. **Day 5 – Give Forgiveness** – Release resentment and offer grace to someone who hurt you.
6. **Day 6 – Give Service** – Volunteer your skills or energy to uplift another.

7. **Day 7 – Give Love** – Perform a simple, intentional act of kindness for someone unexpected.

Goal: To open your life to the flow of abundance by practicing generosity in spirit, word, and deed.

Affirmation to Anchor the Master's Teachings:

"I give freely and joyfully, knowing that abundance flows through me. My generosity opens the door to blessings in my life and the lives of others."

CHAPTER 33

The Search for Purpose: Why Am I Here?

Introduction

Beneath every question lies the deepest one of all: *Why am I here?* The Search for Purpose is not a destination, but a journey inward—a sacred unfolding of soul memory and divine intention. In this intimate dialogue, the Master walks beside the seekers as they explore the call within their hearts, the whispers of their gifts, and the quiet knowing that their life has meaning. Purpose is not found—it is remembered.

Quote

"Your purpose is not something you must chase—it is the light you carry, waiting for you to turn inward and see it clearly."
—The Master

Dialogue: The Seeker and the Master

Seeker (Ethan): Master, I feel lost. I wake up, go to work, come home, and repeat. It's as if I'm living someone else's life. I keep asking myself, why am I here? What is my true purpose?

Master: Ethan, tell me—when a seed is planted in the soil, does it question whether it was meant to be a tree or a flower?

Ethan: No, Master. It simply grows into what it was created to be.

Master: Exactly. You, too, were created with purpose woven into your being. But unlike the seed, man has been given choice. Too often, choice leads to confusion. Instead of growing into what we are meant to be, we chase shadows of what others expect us to be.

Ethan: That is how I feel. I measure myself by my career, my income, and the expectations of others. But deep down, I know that is not my true purpose.

Master: Purpose is not found in titles or possessions. It is discovered at the intersection of three truths:

1. **What you love** – the fire that brings your soul alive.
2. **What you are gifted to do** – the unique abilities placed within you.
3. **How you serve others** – the way your gifts bless the world.

Ethan: So, purpose is not about what I gain, but about what I give?

Master: Yes, Ethan. True purpose always points outward. A life lived only for self will feel empty, no matter the wealth or success. But a life aligned with service will overflow with meaning.

Ethan: Master, what if I still don't know what that is?

Master: Then begin by moving. Purpose rarely reveals itself in stillness. Try, explore, serve, and learn. Every step will bring clarity. And remember—your purpose is not one great destination, but a journey of becoming.

The Master's Compass: Love • Gift • Service

1. **Map Your Loves** – List activities that make you feel *most alive.*
2. **Inventory Your Gifts** – Note strengths others consistently affirm (skills, traits, spiritual gifts).

3. **Choose a Community to Serve** – Who benefits most from your loves and gifts? Be specific.
4. **Design a Small Experiment** – A 30-day pilot (mentor weekly, launch a workshop, serve a team).
5. **Gather Feedback** – Ask those you served what helped most—adjust your focus accordingly.
6. **Write a Purpose Draft** – "My purpose is to serve (people) by (gift) so they can (impact)."
7. **Align Life to Purpose** – Set one 90-day goal, schedule weekly actions, and review progress each Sunday.

Scripture Verse

"For we are His workmanship, created in Christ Jesus for good works, which God prepared beforehand that we should walk in them." – Ephesians 2:10 (NIV)

Reflective Prayer

Heavenly Father,
Thank You for creating me with intention.
When I feel lost, remind me that You have already written purpose into my life.
Open my eyes to see the gifts You have given me,
and give me courage to use them in service to others.
Lead me, step by step, into the life You designed for me,
so that I may live with meaning, joy, and impact.
Amen.

Try This: *10-Day "Walk It Out" Purpose Experiment*

- **Day 1–2:** Complete the Love/Gift/Service lists.
- **Day 3:** Choose one specific community to serve.

- **Day 4:** Draft your purpose sentence.
- **Day 5:** Design a simple 30-day service experiment.
- **Day 6:** Schedule two recurring weekly actions.
- **Day 7–9:** Do the first action(s); ask for real feedback.
- **Day 10:** Reflect and refine your purpose draft and next steps.

Goal: Let movement create clarity—discover purpose by practicing it.

Affirmation to Anchor the Master's Teachings:

"My life has meaning, and I am guided by purpose. Each day, I move closer to the reason I was created, living with intention, passion, and truth."

EPILOGUE

The Journey Beyond the Pages

THE SEEKER ROSE FROM HIS PLACE AT THE FEET OF THE MASTER. The conversations, once simple words, had become living truths in his heart. He no longer carried the same heaviness that had brought him here—though his life was not perfect, his spirit was now anchored in a deeper peace.

He looked back at the garden where their meetings had unfolded. The air seemed lighter, the colors sharper, as though creation itself celebrated the quiet rebirth within him. He whispered to himself, *"I am no longer who I was when I began."*

The Master, seeing his reflection, smiled and spoke:
"This is not the end, but the beginning. Remember, wisdom is a lamp—it lights the path, but you must walk it. The road will stretch long and at times steep, but you are not alone. The same God who carried you to this place will carry you forward. And the voice of truth, once heard, never leaves the heart."

The Seeker bowed, gratitude overflowing. "Then I will walk. And I will keep walking, even when the road bends beyond my sight."

The Master lifted his hand in blessing:
"Walk in faith, walk in courage, walk in love. And wherever your feet touch, let light remain."

And with that, the Seeker stepped forward into his life—not as one burdened by fear, but as one empowered by wisdom, prayer, and grace.

Final Word to the Reader

Beloved reader, you too are the Seeker. These pages were never just about another man's questions, but about your own. The lessons belong to you now. Carry them. Live them. Share them.

For the greatest transformation does not happen when we learn—but when we love, when we give, when we rise, and when we shine.

Your journey continues beyond this book. Step boldly into it.

Scripture Benediction

"The Lord will guide you always;
He will satisfy your needs in a sun-scorched land
and will strengthen your frame.
You will be like a well-watered garden,
like a spring whose waters never fail."
– Isaiah 58:11 (NIV)

AFTERWORD

AS I CLOSE THIS BOOK, I want to pause and thank you—from the depths of my heart—for walking this journey with me.

These chapters were never meant to be just words on a page. They were meant to be seeds. Seeds of faith. Seeds of courage. Seeds of hope. And seeds only fulfill their purpose when they are planted—planted in your heart, your home, your work, your relationships, your prayers.

If you found yourself in the struggles of the Seekers, it is because life will always present us with its valleys and its storms. But it is in those very places that transformation happens. The wisdom of the Master, the prayers at the end of each chapter, and the living Word of Scripture are not distant truths—they are tools you can carry with you each day.

My prayer for you is this: that you do not leave these lessons here, between the covers of this book. Take them with you. Share them. Teach them. And most importantly, *live them*. For the world is waiting for the light you carry, and someone's breakthrough may come because you chose to shine.

Thank you for allowing me to be a companion on your journey. May you walk forward with courage, anchored in wisdom, and covered by grace.

With gratitude,
Willie

Author's Blessing

Beloved reader,
As you lay this book down, may you lift your heart up.

May the wisdom you have received settle deeply into your spirit, guiding your steps with clarity and peace. May the burdens you carried when you opened these pages now feel lighter, replaced with the strength of faith, the courage of truth, and the calm of divine presence.

I bless your mind to be renewed, your heart to be restored, and your life to be realigned with the highest calling God has placed within you. May your relationships flourish with love, your work prospers with purpose, and your path be filled with joy and resilience.

And above all, may you remember that you are never alone. The same Spirit that carried every Seeker in these pages walks with you even now—comforting, teaching, and empowering you.

Go forward, blessed to be a blessing.

"The Lord bless you and keep you;
The Lord make His face shine upon you,
And be gracious to you;
The Lord lift up His countenance upon you,
And give you peace."
—Numbers 6:24–26 (NIV)

With love and light,
Willie

Reader's Prayer

Heavenly Father,
I thank You for the wisdom, lessons, and truths I have received through these pages. I lay my burdens at Your feet—my fears, my doubts, my struggles—and I ask You to renew my mind, refresh my heart, and redirect my steps toward Your will.

Give me the courage to live out what I have learned, the discipline to walk in truth each day, and the humility to grow continually. Strengthen me to overcome avoidance, excuses, and limiting beliefs. Fill me with gratitude, focus, and a deep awareness of my purpose.

Bless my family, my work, my health, and my relationships, so that all I do may reflect Your light. Teach me to lead with love, to serve with joy, and to honor You with the gifts You have given me.

Today, I choose to move forward—not in my strength alone, but in Yours. May my life be a living testimony of faith, hope, and love.

In Jesus' name, Amen.

Scripture to Anchor This Prayer

"I can do all things through Christ who strengthens me." —
Philippians 4:13(NIV)

Share your accomplishment and transformation with others.

ABOUT THE AUTHOR

Willie C. Hooks is more than a coach and consultant—he is a guide who has walked the road of struggle, resilience, and faith himself. Raised by a single mother alongside three brothers, Willie learned early the value of discipline, hard work, and holding on to hope even in the toughest of times. From cutting grass as a young boy to becoming a trusted advisor to business leaders and community builders, his journey has always been about transformation—first his own, and then the lives of those he serves.

For decades, Willie has mentored leaders, executives, and everyday seekers, blending practical wisdom with spiritual truth. His mission is to help people break free from limiting beliefs, embrace their God-given purpose, and create lives filled with clarity, courage, and balance.

In *Under the Fig Tree*, Willie opens the same sacred space he has created for countless seekers—sharing wisdom, stories, and tools that bring light to life's challenges and clarity to life's purpose. This book is both a reflection of his personal journey and an invitation to yours.

OTHER BOOKS BY WILLIE C. HOOKS

THE ABILITY TO RAISE MONEY is a critical skill that will support you in achieving greater success and in building financial wealth much faster. Regardless of the business that you are in, or the project that you are pursuing, you will need money and financial resources to capture that business opportunity. It is so obvious when you take the time to think about it that all ideas, businesses and financial opportunities require money to be realized.

IN THIS COMPETITIVE WORLD, if you are not increasing your personal effectiveness each day then you are moving backwards because you are losing some of the effectiveness that is the key to maintaining a competitive advantage in this dynamic global market. The Personal Effectiveness Toolkit is filled with tips and techniques that are guaranteed to increase your performance, results, and ultimately your success in whatever profession, business, or competitive arena you are operating in.

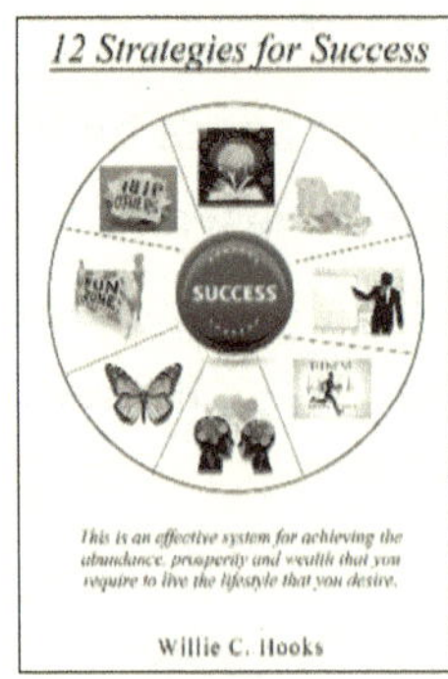

ARE YOU AT A POINT IN YOUR LIFE where you have unfulfilled dreams and aspirations? Perhaps you can even visualize the lifestyle that you desire. However you don't have a systematic approach that allows you to consistently take action and make progress toward your goals. This book provides 12 effective and implementable strategies that will put you on the path to creating the abundance, prosperity, and wealth required to live the lifestyle that you desire. You will discover: -How to live a balanced life.

NOTES

NOTES

NOTES

NOTES

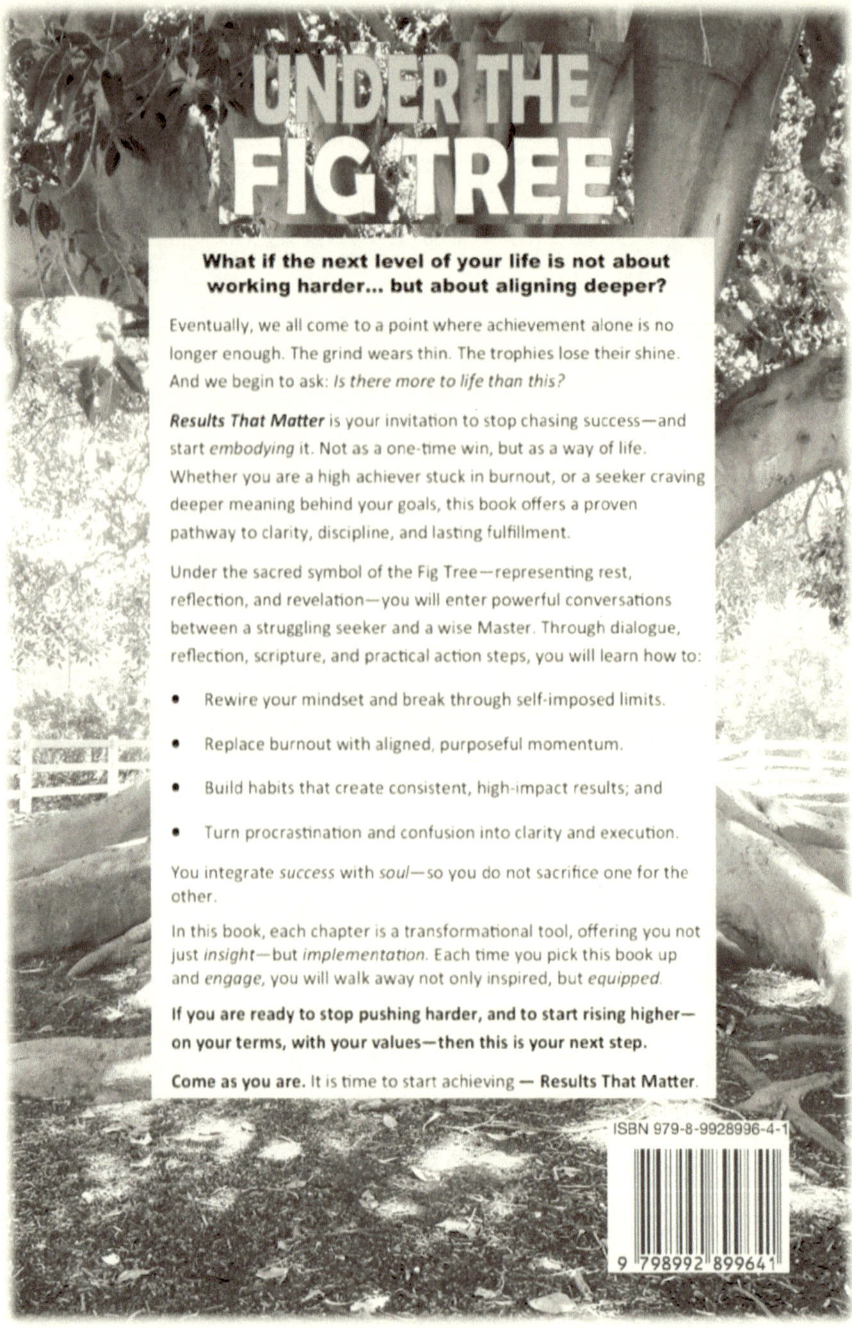
UNDER THE
FIG TREE
What if the next level of your life is not about working harder... but about aligning deeper?
Eventually, we all come to a point where achievement alone is no longer enough. The grind wears thin. The trophies lose their shine. And we begin to ask: Is there more to life than this?
Results That Matter is your invitation to stop chasing success—and start embodying it. Not as a one-time win, but as a way of life. Whether you are a high achiever stuck in burnout, or a seeker craving deeper meaning behind your goals, this book offers a proven pathway to clarity, discipline, and lasting fulfillment.
Under the sacred symbol of the Fig Tree—representing rest, reflection, and revelation—you will enter powerful conversations between a struggling seeker and a wise Master. Through dialogue, reflection, scripture, and practical action steps, you will learn how to:
• Rewire your mindset and break through self-imposed limits.
• Replace burnout with aligned, purposeful momentum.
• Build habits that create consistent, high-impact results; and
• Turn procrastination and confusion into clarity and execution.
You integrate success with soul—so you do not sacrifice one for the other.
In this book, each chapter is a transformational tool, offering you not just insight—but implementation. Each time you pick this book up and engage, you will walk away not only inspired, but equipped.
If you are ready to stop pushing harder, and to start rising higher—on your terms, with your values—then this is your next step.
Come as you are. It is time to start achieving — Results That Matter.
ISBN 979-8-9928996-4-1
9 798992 899641

www.ingramcontent.com/pod-product-compliance
Lightning Source LLC
LaVergne TN
LVHW090607110826
845146LV00001B/299